Determinants of Animal

CW00687440

Are animals intelligent? How do they learn to solve everyday survival problems? Can they be intentionally deceptive? The investigation of animal intelligence and behaviour is an important and fascinating aspect of comparative psychology. This book thoroughly covers the section on determinants of animal behaviour in the AQA(A) comparative psychology module and deals with the three main topics featured in the syllabus. First, the evolutionary explanations of animal behaviour are discussed, including the biological explanations of apparent altruism. Second, the nature of classical and operant conditioning in animal behaviour is considered. Finally, the role of social learning in animals is investigated.

Determinants of Animal Behaviour is an ideal introductory text to the subject, full of real-life examples and both traditional and cutting-edge research. It will be of interest to all students new to comparative psychology and highly accessible to anyone wishing to know more about the diversity and ingenuity of animal behaviour.

Jo-Anne Cartwright is an experienced A-Level teacher and examiner for the AQA examination board.

Routledge Modular Psychology

Series editors: Cara Flanagan is a Reviser for AS and A2 level Psychology and is an experienced author and teacher. Philip Banyard is Associate Senior Lecturer in Psychology at Nottingham Trent University and a Chief Examiner for AS and A2 level Psychology. Both are experienced writers.

The *Routledge Modular Psychology* series is a completely new approach to introductory level psychology, tailor-made to the new modular style of teaching. Each short book covers a topic in more detail than any large textbook can, allowing teacher and student to select material exactly to suit any particular course or project.

The books have been written especially for those students new to higher-level study, whether at school, college or university. They include specially designed features to help with technique, such as a model essay at an average level with an examiner's comments to show how extra marks can be gained. The authors are all examiners and teachers at the introductory level.

The *Routledge Modular Psychology* texts are all user-friendly and accessible and include the following features:

- practice essays with specialist commentary to show how to achieve a higher grade
- chapter summaries to assist with revision
- progress and review exercises
- glossary of key terms
- summaries of key research
- further reading to stimulate ongoing study and research
- cross-referencing to other books in the series

Also available in this series (titles listed by syllabus section):

To all of my family, and friends, especially my son Scott, my daughter Paris, my husband Alan, my mum Denise and dad Edmond, because without their unconditional love and support my life would be completely meaningless

Determinants of
Animal Behaviour

Jo-Anne Cartwright

First published 2002 by Routledge
27 Church Road, Hove, East Sussex, BN3 2FA

Simultaneously published in the USA and Canada
by Routledge
29 West 35th Street, New York, NY 10001

Routledge is an imprint of the Taylor & Francis Group

© 2002 Psychology Press

Typeset in Times and Frutiger by Keystroke,
Jacaranda Lodge, Wolverhampton
Printed and bound in Great Britain
by TJ International Ltd,
Padstow, Cornwall

Cover design by Terry Foley

All rights reserved. No part of this book may be reprinted or
reproduced or utilised in any form or by any electronic, mechanical,
or other means, now known or hereafter invented, including
photocopying and recording, or in any information storage or
retrieval system, without permission in writing from the publishers.

British Library Cataloguing in Publication Data
A catalogue record for this book is available from the British Library

Library of Congress Cataloging in Publication Data
Cartwright, Jo-Anne, 1955–
    Determinants of animal behaviour / Jo-Anne Cartwright.
        p. cm.—(Routledge modular psychology)
    Includes bibliographical references and index.
    ISBN 0–415–23840–4—ISBN 0–415–23841–2 (pbk.)
    1. Psychology, Comparative. I. Title. II. Series.

BF671 .C37 2002
591.5—dc21   2001048494

ISBNs 0–415–23841–2 (pbk)
0–415–23840–4 (hbk)

Contents

Illustrations

Figures

Tables

Preface

This book has primarily been written for A-level and undergraduate psychology students. However, it should be equally stimulating for a wide variety of people. For example, those who are interested in learning more about our evolutionary ancestors, those who are interested in discovering the amazingly diverse ways that animals solve their everyday survival problems such as territorial behaviour, how they learn, how they have evolved into the many different species, etc. Those studying zoology and/or animal behaviour and those who simply want to know more about animal behaviour in general.

The main intentions of this book are fivefold. To convey to the reader how fascinating and diverse the behaviour of those creatures we share this planet with is. To give the reader a flavour of the depth and diversity of knowledge and understanding that has been assembled about non-human animal behaviour. To show how studying non-human animal behaviour may help us to gain an understanding of human behaviour. To convince the band of sceptics, to which I once belonged, who see no point or value in studying animal behaviour, that the study of non-human animal behaviour is essential for gaining a complete understanding of human behaviour. Finally, it is to encourage humans to respect their evolutionary ancestors in all their forms. Nevertheless, there is one other intention – that, if nothing else the reader should enjoy reading this book.

Acknowledgements

I must acknowledge those people (and there have been many along the way) who have enabled me to develop the knowledge, the understanding and the skills of research to write this book.

The Welsh wizard, Byron Edwards, who has taken a great deal of sarcasm from me over the years for his dogged (sorry for the pun) belief that non-human animals are a valuable source for understanding human behaviour, and who eventually convinced me of the merits of his argument.

All at Routledge involved in the production of this book, especially Cara Flanagan who offered me much needed advice and guidance throughout.

Last, but certainly not least, my husband, family and friends who have endured my unsociable behaviour during the many hours it has taken to research and write this book. However, they may well encourage me to write another book when they realise that I am able to spend more time with them!

Acknowledgements

1

Introduction

 What is non-human animal behaviour?
Why study animal behaviour?
How do we study animal behaviour?
Summary

What is non-human animal behaviour?

Simply defined, non-human animal behaviour is anything an animal does - its feeding habits, its reproductive conduct, the way it rears its young, and a host of other activities. Behaviour is the whole animal's adjustment to changes inside its body or in its environment and is always an organised action.

The group activities of non-human animals (hereafter referred to as animals) are an important aspect of animal behaviour. For example, bees communicate with each other about sources of food, and birds may flock during migratory flights. Group activities are often adaptations to a new set of circumstances; without **adaptation** (any structural or behavioural change that increases the probability that an animal will survive) a species could not survive in their ever-changing environment.

Behaviour can also be thought of as a response to a **stimulus** (something which stimulates the senses), whether it involves a change in the body or a change in the environment. All animals, even those too small to be seen without a microscope, respond to stimuli.

Why study animal behaviour?

One very good reason for studying animal behaviour is because the creatures we share our planet with are fascinating in their own right. Indeed, people have studied animals for thousands of years. Ancient humans studied animals, and while this was primarily to hunt and domesticate them they also studied them because they were curious about them. Nevertheless there are much more serious reasons for studying animal behaviour and, for some, it has become a scientific speciality to try to find out *why* animals behave the way that they do; and *how* their behaviour may help them and their offspring survive in their particular environmental niche (corner).

Just like humans, animals use their freedom to move and interact with their environment and with one another in a bid to try to solve their survival problems – for example, in finding and obtaining food; in avoiding becoming another animal's meal; in finding, obtaining and keeping a suitable mate and a suitable 'home'; and in rearing viable offspring. These are just a few of the survival problems faced by animals and humans.

The role of evolution in animal behaviour

Evolution appears to have forged each species' behaviour, resulting in distinct species adopting different strategies for solving their survival problems and, to some extent, each individual adopting their own ways of solving their survival problems. Animals are therefore studied in a bid to understand how they adapt to their environment and in order to recognise what strategies they have evolved (developed) to solve their survival problems. This, of course, includes human animals, and if we accept Darwin's proposal in his theory of evolution that all living organisms evolved from the same simple organisms then, to some extent, animals and humans must have a number of shared behaviours. Furthermore, many scientists claim that humans and modern apes shared the same common ancestor. If we accept what biologists tell us – that is, that the DNA difference between humans and our chimpanzee cousins is only 1.4 (meaning that chimpanzees share 98.6 per cent of the human genome) – then there must be a great number of similarities between humans and chimpanzees than there are differences.

Through studying animals it may be possible to determine what we humans have in common with our animal (evolutionary) ancestors and what we do not have in common. For example, we may learn a route from our house to a given location and back again. Similarly, some animals must learn the route from their home and back again when they go on foraging trips; or, more astounding, when they migrate over thousands of miles and return to precisely the same place that they left months or years before.

These considerations raise a number of questions that should be addressed. Are humans qualitatively different from animals or simply quantitatively different? For example, do humans have some qualities (e.g. language, intelligence and consciousness) that animals do not? Or are the differences between humans and animals simply quantitative, whereby we share the same qualities (e.g. intelligence) but in different amounts? These, in turn, raise many more questions about behaviour; for example, do animals and humans learn things in the same way and, if not, how do they differ? Were our closest evolutionary ancestors (*Homo habilis*, an ancient form of ape) intelligent in similar ways to us humans but simply had less of 'it'? Or did they have a very different kind of intelligence to humans? These and the multitude of questions raised by considering whether humans and animals are qualitatively or quantitatively different can only truly be answered by studying animal behaviour.

Benefits gained from studying animal behaviour

Another good reason for studying animal behaviour is because it can result in benefits for both humans and animals. For example, research on animals' sensory systems has led to practical applications that have benefited human and animals – consider the examples which follow.

Griffin's (1992) research on bats' sonar abilities indirectly led to the development and use of sonar techniques to benefit both humans and animals. For example, the ultrasound scanner used to detect the development of foetuses in the womb and to spot any problems long before birth. Sonar systems have also been developed to enable large shipping to detect schools of dolphins in order to avoid them.

Pavlov's pioneering research on **classical conditioning** (covered in Chapter 3), that established many principles of learning, has led to the application of learning principles in human medicine, such as over-coming the detrimental consequences of chemotherapy or radiation treatment for patients being treated for cancer (Bernstein, 1991). One of the unfortunate side effects of these treatments is nausea and vomiting. This particular side effect occurs because not only does the treatment kill the rapidly dividing cancer cells but it also kills the rapidly dividing cells that line the digestive system, consequently resulting in nausea and vomiting. Pavlov's pioneering research has led to the knowledge that if a cancer patient is given a particular food just prior to receiving treatment they unconsciously associate the food with the nausea and vomiting, even though they consciously know it is the treatment that is causing it. This unconscious association formed between the food and the sickness causes patients to develop an aversion to the food eaten prior to treatment. As a nutritious diet is vital for aiding recovery, knowledge of this inappropriate association has resulted in these patients being given only non-nutritious food prior to the treatment; the result is that patients develop an aversion to the non-nutritious food and not to the nutritious food.

Pavlov's pioneering research has also led to other benefits for animals, as the same taste-aversion principles found in cancer patients have been employed for saving endangered species. For example, some species of turtle have been endangered because mongooses have been eating their eggs. However, putting an emetic (i.e. something that makes the animal vomit) in some of the turtles' eggs and letting the mongooses eat these has led to them avoiding these turtles' eggs; this has resulted in a significant increase in these turtle populations (Nicolaus and Nellis, 1987).

Animals may also be studied for other reasons – for example, when it would be unethical and/or impractical to use humans, such as in experimental research involving the effects of early loss of the mother, or the effect of permanent damage to the brain or other vital organs. Animals are also used because they reproduce and develop much faster than humans do, making it easier to study genetic inheritance and environmental effects. Consequently it can be seen that there are a number of valid reasons for studying animal behaviour.

How do we study animal behaviour?

When we study animal behaviour we look at what animals do in different circumstances and we try to find explanations for particular behaviour patterns. There are a number of methods for studying animal behaviour. It can be studied by systematically observing and recording their behaviour in a natural setting (normal habitat). On the other hand, it can be observed in a highly controlled laboratory setting where some things can be held constant (such as temperature, light) while systematically changing others (such as hormone levels) – or by a combination of these two, therefore observing animals in a natural setting but systematically changing aspects of their environment.

The ethological method of studying animal behaviour

The systematic observation of an animal's behaviour in its natural setting is called **ethology**. The ethological method of research is mainly used to establish the function (purpose) of an animal's behaviour. Ethology stresses the importance of studying behaviour in its natural setting, involving systematically observing and recording the ways in which animals solve their survival problems in their natural environment; for example, systematically observing and recording nest-building and egg-laying behaviour in birds.

Ethologists also carry out simple experiments which involve systematically changing aspects of the animals' natural environment; for example, systematically observing and recording nest-building and egg-laying behaviour in birds and also placing another bird's egg in some of these birds' nests but not others. These simple experiments are called field experiments, and are usually carried out to make the relationship between a specific behaviour and the behaviour's apparent function (purpose) or functions clear.

The ethological method of research has an advantage over the experimental method in that it will usually observe behaviour that represents the animal's normal actions because the animal is in its natural habitat. Nevertheless, because the researcher has no real control over the situation it is not possible to establish precisely what caused the animal's behaviour. Consequently, this lack of control of the situation may result in an inappropriate conclusion being drawn about the relationship between a specific behaviour and the behaviour's apparent function (purpose) or functions.

The laboratory experimental method of studying animal behaviour

In contrast to the ethological method, the laboratory approach to studying animal behaviour involves systematically observing it in a highly controlled laboratory setting to try to establish the precise cause of the behaviour. This method allows the researcher to have explicit control over the situation, enabling all aspects of the environment to be kept the same, apart from those which are required to be changed. Clearly then, if what is changed results in a change in the animal's behaviour, and everything else remains the same, the researcher can be more sure that what was changed in the animals environment was the cause of the change in behaviour. Furthermore, because of the highly controlled, precise nature of the laboratory the experiment can easily be replicated to see whether findings are reliable (highly similar each time); this is not the case when using the ethological method.

Consequently, the use of the experimental method (unlike the ethological method) means that researchers can be more confident about the conclusions of the causes of behaviours. Nevertheless, because these animals are being studied in a highly unnatural situation, then findings gained using this method may not represent animals' behaviour in its natural environment. This may therefore render the conclusions about the cause and/or function of the animals' behaviour inappropriate in relation to the real world.

However, while these two methods are very different ways of studying animal behaviour they are not independent of each other. Instead, comparative psychologists adopt both methods in order to establish the functions of behaviour and the causes of behaviour, therefore gaining a more complete understanding of animal behaviour.

Points to note when studying animal behaviour

Before we consider what research into animal behaviour has taught us about human and animal behaviour there are three important points that should be noted:

- The problem of **anthropomorphism**.
- Avoiding taking information at face value.
- The Law of Parsimony (Lloyd Morgan's canon).

The problem of anthropomorphism

Over the years a great deal of fanciful animal folklore has arisen. This has often led to the mistaken belief that animals behave in particular ways for the same reasons that humans do – for example, because they are angry, frustrated, puzzled, happy, etc. Adopting such a stance is to commit the 'sin' of anthropomorphism; that is, attributing animals with the same qualities as humans. Anthropomorphism can clearly be seen in the passage written in the first century by the famous Roman author Pliny the Elder:

> The largest land animal is the elephant. It is the nearest to man in intelligence; it understands the language of its country and obeys orders, remembers duties that it has been taught, is pleased by affection and by marks of honor, nay more it possesses virtues rare even for man, honesty, wisdom, justice, also respect for the stars and reverence for the sun and moon.

While most animal researchers and lay people would never deny that the elephant could be taught to perform certain tasks, no one today would seriously believe that all of Pliny's other claims are true.

Anthropomorphism is still seen today; for instance, a present-day example of anthropomorphism is clearly apparent on the website of the Hawaii Whale Research Foundation where it discusses breaching behaviour (see below) in humpback whales. Some of the information on this web page can be used to show how anthropomorphism can easily influence a researcher's thoughts and muddy once impartial observations and interpretations.

A breach refers to the whale breaking through the surface of the water and leaping vertically into the air, out of its natural element. It is probably the most hoped-to-be-seen behaviour among whale watchers. Other whale species breach more often, but none so dramatically as the humpback. A full breach involves the humpback whale leaping completely (or almost completely) out of the water. It can rise above the water almost as high as it is long – up to 45 feet. As it falls, the whale usually assumes a horizontal position so that it hits the water laid out flat (a belly flop). Now consider the following comments made by a researcher on the Hawaii Whale Research Foundation's web page:

> Sometimes a whale that has just become active (after apparently resting), has just left a social group, or is excited or irritated will perform a series of breaches.

Breaching is often interpreted as a show of playfulness by a whale. Such an interpretation is likely incorrect and an example of anthropomorphism, where human characteristics are attributed to animals. In fact, while we do not know why a breach is performed, it may signal that the whale is anything but playful.

As the researcher quite rightly points out, referring to breaching as a show of playfulness is anthropomorphism; however, the researcher's previous comments also suffer from anthropomorphism when she or he states 'is excited or irritated'.

Anthropomorphism is therefore easily attributed without conscious thought and is often very difficult to avoid. The trend regarding anthropomorphism is that researchers should try to avoid it at all costs as it may lead to inappropriate conclusions about animal behaviour. Anthropomorphism may also prevent us from becoming aware that animal experience may be very different to human experience, and may result in us overlooking aspects of their behaviour. Nevertheless, some researchers argue that this extreme stance on avoidance of anthropomorphism may result in researchers drawing inappropriate conclusions about animal behaviour because they are denying animals some behaviours that they may well possess.

The following quote from Sue Savage-Rumbaugh (1994) clearly sums up the need for unbiased, valid and reliable animal research:

> We do not realise how deeply our starting assumptions affect the way we go about looking for and interpreting the data we collect. We should recognize that non-human organisms need not meet every new definition of tool use, mind or consciousness in order to have versions of their own that are worthy of serious study. We have set ourselves too much apart, grasping for definitions that will distinguish man from all other life on the planet. We must rejoin the great stream of life from whence we arose and strive to see within it the seeds of all we are and all we may become.
>
> (Savage-Rumbaugh, 1994: 264)

Avoiding taking information at face value

It is vital that we do not take information at face value. Just because something is written in a textbook and is stated by researchers, scientists, theorists, professors, etc., does not mean it must be so. Therefore always question what you read, considering things like does the research have ecological validity (represent real-life behaviour), or does it represent artificial behaviour? Is the research methodology appropriate in relation to what is supposed to be being studied? Is the evidence reliable? And so forth. Remember nonsense is nonsense however it is 'dressed up'. Also remember that knowledge established in its day may not be acceptable either today and/or in the future – consider it was once strongly believed that the world was flat!

The Law of Parsimony (Lloyd Morgan's canon)

There are a number of ways of explaining animal behaviour, and these range from the complex to the simple. Therefore, if we observe a cat getting out of Thorndike's puzzle box (covered in Chapter 3), by pulling a loop of string that is attached, via a pulley wheel, to the door of the puzzle box, thus causing the door to be raised and, consequently, enabling the cat to get out, we can explain its behaviour by stating that the cat had an understanding of the mechanisms of the box and 'knew' how to get out. Alternatively, we can explain the cat's behaviour by stating that the cat has simply learned an association between pulling the loop and getting out of the puzzle box and has no conscious knowledge or understanding of how it achieved this feat. The first explanation is much more complex than the second one. The first explanation also makes the most assumptions as it assumes that the cat has some complex thought processes; the latter explanation, however, does not make any such assumption. According to the Law of Parsimony (also known as Lloyd Morgan's canon) explanations of animal behaviour should always use the least complex level of explanation that makes the least assumptions. Therefore in the case of the cat escaping from the puzzle box we should adopt the second explanation, and should not assume that animals have complex mental processes unless we are unable to explain behaviour in any other way.

Summary

There are many reasons why we study animal behaviour. They are interesting in their own right; they can also help us understand what humans have evolved from and can lead to practical applications that can benefit both humans and animals. Nevertheless, we must be wary of assuming that the cause of animal behaviour is the same as it is for a human; that is, we must avoid anthropomorphism at all costs when studying animal behaviour. We must also question everything and not simply take information at face value. And, finally, we must adhere to the Law of Parsimony wherever possible.

2

Evolutionary explanations of animal behaviour

An introduction to evolutionary theory

In the context of determinants of animal behaviour, **evolution** refers to gradual, relatively orderly changes in the genetic composition of an animal population, from one generation to another. Therefore, evolution is a gradual process of genetic modification whereby the genetic characteristics of a whole species are changed over many generations, causing a physical and/or behavioural variation that serves to adapt individuals more adequately to their **environmental niche**. Consequently, on a large scale evolution may involve the appearance, disappearance, and/or transformation of whole species, over long spans of time. However, on a smaller scale it may involve the appearance, disappearance or transformation of specific characteristics of individuals within a species.

It should be understood that due to the genetic rearrangement that occurs as a result of sexual reproduction (or much less often through mutation), each animal's genetic make-up differs slightly from the genetic make-up of its parents. Hence while all members of a species may have a number of the same characteristics, and/or exhibit the same behaviours, each individual may have characteristics and/or behaviours that are unique to them.

A basic introduction to evolutionary theory

It should be known that evolution is a *fact* not a theory; however, many theories have been proposed to try to explain how and why evolution occurs, the most influential one being Darwin's theory of evolution.

Darwin's theory is based on the assumption that, in the natural state of affairs, there is competition for limited resources (e.g. food, water, mates, etc.) in the environment. Darwin's theory states that evolution occurs due to **natural selection**. What Darwin means by natural selection is that nature will 'favour' those organisms that have greater **fitness**. Fitness simply refers to the ability to survive long enough to produce viable offspring (i.e. offspring that are likely to also survive long enough to also reproduce). Consequently, animals that have inherited characteristics that increase the probability that they will produce viable offspring have greater fitness than those who do not inherit such characteristics; therefore, nature will not favour those organisms that have lesser fitness. The animals with the greater fitness will increase in number because most of their offspring will have also inherited these characteristics and they, in turn, will produce offspring who will also produce offspring, and so on. Animals with lesser fitness will decrease in number because they are less likely (than the animals with greater fitness) to survive long enough to reproduce successfully. And even if the animals with the least fitness do reproduce, these offspring are also less likely to survive long enough to produce viable offspring. In short, nature favours animals that have greater fitness, this being related to inherited characteristics that have enabled a species to survive and reproduce successfully in the environment that it inhabits. Consequently, both inherited characteristics and environmental conditions determine fitness.

The following example will make these claims a little clearer. Suppose that members of a given species (for example, birds) have all inherited the attribute 'beak', and that individuals within the species vary slightly, resulting in a range of beaks in terms of size and strength.

Now further suppose that half of these birds are living in an 'insect environment', where there is a plentiful supply of insects found deep inside tubular flowers but not a lot else to eat, and that the other half of these birds are living in a 'nut environment', where there is a plentiful supply of hard-shelled nuts but not much else. Eating is necessary for survival and those most likely to survive in the 'insect environment' are going to be those with long, thin beaks which can reach down inside the flowers; those who cannot reach the food will die. However, those most likely to survive in the 'nut environment' are those with big, strong beaks which can be used to crack the nuts; those who cannot will die. Thus, the ones with the characteristics most likely to enhance their survival in a given situation will be the ones left to reproduce, hence passing their characteristics on to the next generation through **genetic transmission**. Furthermore, each generation may have individuals who have an even better-suited beak for the environment; others will have a worse-suited beak. Consequently, the better the beak is suited to the environment then the greater the probability that the birds will survive and produce offspring, resulting in an increase in birds with these beaks; conversely the worse suited a beak is to the environment the less the probability that they will survive long enough to produce offspring, resulting in a decrease in birds with these beaks. Ultimately these small changes in beak size and strength may lead to the evolution of a new species through the process of natural selection.

Several conclusions can be drawn from the above example.

Evolution does not require an animal to 'know' what it needs to do in order to survive, it simply has to behave in ways that will ensure that it leaves viable offspring.

An animal's behaviours are often biologically crucial to its survival, and hence reproductive success, therefore we should expect any behaviour exhibited to reflect the degree of reproductive success.

Reproductive success is the crucial factor in evolution as survival is only relevant because it increases the probability of successfully reproducing viable offspring. To make this point clearer, consider the following. An animal that spends its time successfully gaining food and avoiding predators, which does not engage in mate-seeking or reproductive behaviour, may well survive for a relatively long time, but its genes would not be represented in the next generation. Consequently, for all its efforts, its survival in terms of genetic transmission would be very short in comparison to those that did reproduce, clearly implying that adaptive behaviour (fitness) relies on an individual being able to produce viable offspring.

Genetic and environmental determinants of behaviour

Behaviour is determined by a combination of both the individual's **nature**, through genetic transmission (i.e. the combined genes inherited from mother and father), and its **nurture**, through environmental factors. The genetic transmission is a function of the organism's **genotype**, expressed in the **phenotype**. A genotype is simply the specific genetic material that an individual organism has inherited, as opposed to a phenotype that is simply the physical and behaviour characteristics the individual actually displays; an individual's phenotype is due to the influence of both the genotype and the environment. An example should make the difference between phenotype and genotype clearer. Identical twins have the same genotype. Let us suppose that in the genotype of one pair of twins there is a gene for high intelligence. Further consider that this pair of twins are separated at birth and reared in two different environments: one in an enriched environment where mental stimulation is plentiful (lots of books, encouragement, discussion, etc.), the other twin in a deprived environment where such mental stimulation is very scarce. These environmental differences would cause them to have very different phenotypes of intelligence: the enriched twin would be much more intelligent than the deprived twin is, even though both had identical genotypes that included a gene for high intelligence. Therefore whether or not an organism's genotype is reflected in its phenotype is dependent on environmental influences. (NB genes *cannot* be changed by environmental influences; instead, the changes in an organism's genetically determined characteristics are the result of different combinations of genes being passed on to the next generation through genetic transmission, and not through changes in the genes themselves.)

Applying the theory of evolution

The theory of evolution has been used to explain a vast number of behaviours. We will consider two of them: evolutionary explanations of apparent **altruism** and evolutionary explanations of territorial behaviour – known as territoriality.

Introduction to altruism

Altruism can be defined as behaviour that promotes the welfare or survival of others (benefits) but simultaneously places those performing such behaviours at risk from harm (costs). It can also be defined as acts that result in great benefits for those receiving it but at great cost to those performing the altruistic act. Consequently, altruism is a social behaviour that involves an animal performing an act that apparently *increases* another animal's chances of survival while seemingly *decreasing* its own. For example, a rabbit raises the alarm when a predator approaches. This consequently brings attention to the alarm-raising rabbit yet detracts attention away from other rabbits, giving them a chance to escape from the predator. Altruism is therefore the ultimate form of 'helping', as the animal places itself in a situation that involves *costs* to the altruist (the one performing the altruistic act) and *benefits* to the recipients of altruism. Such behaviour appears to be exactly what natural selection would oppose. This is because by performing an act that places their own survival at risk in order to enhance others' survival, the altruist may lose the future opportunity to reproduce and, consequently, might produce fewer offspring than the non-altruists would.

Acts of human altruism abound in real life – for example, kidney donors, adoptive parents, heroes, etc. Such altruistic acts are clearly a **paradox** (contradiction), as far as Darwin's theory is concerned, because if an altruist puts its own life at risk then it risks losing any chance of producing viable offspring; consequently, altruism is of great interest to scientists. Darwin's theory of evolution states that natural selection can only favour adaptations that cause an animal to produce more offspring. Therefore it should favour selfishness, because this would enhance an animal's survival and thus reproductive success. However, on the face of it, altruism appears to do just the opposite.

Recall the example of variation in beaks, whereby the genes responsible for inappropriate beaks would eventually disappear as possessors of these genes become less and less numerous. This, according to the principles of natural selection, is what should happen to altruists; that is, altruists should eventually become less and less numerous and eventually die out because this behaviour results in lesser fitness than non-altruistic behaviour. In sum, by the principles of natural selection, non-altruists should come to prevail in all natural populations.

Human altruism has therefore stumped biologists for centuries and has inspired them to search the animal kingdom for signs of similar behaviour among animals to try to either explain why altruism does exist when, according to Darwin's theory of evolution, it should not, or to establish whether altruism truly exists.

Does altruism exist in the animal kingdom?

The answer to this question appears to be a resounding 'yes', as it would appear that altruism does exist in the animal kingdom. Some examples of animal altruism will now be considered.

Belding's ground squirrel is a small mammal that forms breeding colonies containing many burrows high in the Rocky Mountains (Sherman, 1977). When a predator such as a fox or a hawk appears it seems that the first squirrel to spot it generally gives an alarm call. When the other squirrels in the vicinity hear the alarm call they commonly stop what they are doing and either scan their environment to establish the location of the predator or simply dive for cover into their burrows. Thus the squirrel raising the alarm brings its existence and location to the attention of the predator, consequently decreasing the probability that it will survive while simultaneously alerting the other squirrels and increasing the probability that they will survive. In sum, decreasing the animal's fitness.

In many species of birds (e.g. the Florida scrub jay *Aphelocoma coerulescens*) the offspring of earlier broods remain with the parents after the fledgling stage to help their parents rear the next broods, which are of course their biological brothers and sisters (Mumme, 1992). Hence these 'remaining' birds are forfeiting their chance to produce their own offspring. An extreme form of altruism is seen in social insects (ants, bees, wasps and termites), whereby some 'worker' individuals are completely sterile and devote all of their energies to rearing the offspring of other individuals. Probably the most extreme form of altruism can be seen in the stinging behaviour of bees. The sting, once inserted into its victim, cannot be removed. This results in the bee's abdomen being wrenched from its body and therefore the death of the individual bee. Nevertheless, the hive mates will benefit from this sacrifice because it may deter others from approaching their nest site and the nest site of other bees.

Evolutionary explanations of apparent altruism

It should now be clear that natural selection would not favour the selection of altruism, yet altruism exists and continues to exist – that is the paradox. This paradox has elicited four main types of evolutionary explanation – *group selection theory*, *kin selection theory*, *reciprocal altruism theory* and *manipulated altruism* – but only the final three are convincing. These explanations will now be considered and evaluated.

Group selection theory (Wynne-Edwards, 1962)

So far we have supposed, as Darwin did, that natural selection works at the individual level, in that natural selection only produces adaptations that enhance an individual's reproductive success. That is, an individual that has high levels of fitness is far more likely to produce viable offspring than an individual that has low levels of fitness. Accordingly, Darwin's theory proposes that if group adaptation (fitness) is the same as an individual's adaptation then this is merely a lucky coincidence. The theory of group selection reverses this proposal and states that natural selection operates at the group level as well as at the individual level.

According to the group selection model, a group that has the greatest fitness – that is, the group that has characteristics that increase the probability that the group will survive long enough to produce viable offspring – will be more successful than a group that has lesser fitness. The theory also claims that gradually all members of a species will, as a group, come to share favourable characteristics. An example should make group selection theory's claims clearer. Dense populations of animals have come about because there is an abundance of required resources (enrichment) in the environment. Conversely, sparse populations have come about because there is a shortage of required resources (impoverishment) in the environment. Impoverishment of an environment can occur for many reasons, such as a dense population using resources or climate changes, and environments that change from enriched to impoverished exert evolutionary pressure as there are no longer sufficient resources for the group. Group selection theory claims that while the group's least fittest members (in this case altruists) will die off, and the fittest will survive and produce viable offspring, the benefit of having altruists in the group is because it increases the overall fitness of the group. This is why group selection claims that natural selection operates at the group level and not, as Darwin proposed, at the individual level. Consequently, group selection states that natural selection will favour characteristics that decrease the probability that the group will become extinct.

According to group selection altruism is just one of a number of characteristics that favour the group rather than the individual and therefore it can be expected to evolve if natural selection does indeed work at group rather than individual level.

An evaluation of group selection theory

Does natural selection operate at the group level? Initially it would seem that natural selection does appear to operate at the group rather than the individual level. This seems especially appropriate for altruism as it appears that altruism incurs no obvious or immediate benefits for the individual (indeed just the opposite) but instead appears to benefit the group. Let us reconsider the earlier example of the rabbit that warns fellow rabbits of an approaching predator. This would increase the fitness of the group of rabbits but not the individual rabbit's fitness, as by alerting fellow rabbits it draws attention to itself, consequently informing the predator of its whereabouts. Nevertheless, it has been found that the conditions under which group selection would work are so restrictive that they would probably rarely, if ever, be realised in the real world. Consequently group selection can be ruled out, because in principle it is unworkable. This is because natural selection is probably far more powerful at producing adaptations that increase an individual's success at producing viable offspring than it is at producing adaptations that increase a group's reproductive success. The reason for this is probably because the turnover of individuals is far higher than that of groups. Furthermore, we do not need this theory because the three remaining evolutionary explanations appear to account for altruistic behaviour far more effectively. These three will now be considered.

Kin selection theory

The most prominent of the three remaining explanations of altruism is kin selection theory, proposed by W. D. Hamilton (1964). Kin selection theory proposes that those selected to receive altruistic acts will be kin (i.e. blood relatives). This theory claims that natural selection does not favour individual fitness (the reproductive success of an individual); instead it favours **inclusive fitness** (the reproductive success of those individuals who share the same genes). Consequently, kin selection theory claims that natural selection operates at the genetic level, and not, as Darwin suggested, at the individual level. Therefore kin selection theory sees reproductive success as simply successfully passing one's genes into the next generation. Kin selection theory therefore predicts that kin (blood relatives) are more likely to receive altruism because they share the same genes as the altruist. Accordingly, if altruism is shown to others that share the altruist's genes, then by increasing blood relatives' reproductive success the altruist's reproductive success is also increased. This is because altruism increases the chances of the recipient's survival and therefore increases the probability that genes, shared by altruist and recipient, will successfully pass into the next generation.

Evidence for kin selection theory

If kin selection theory is correct we would expect that the majority of altruistic acts will be directed at close blood relatives (e.g. brothers, sisters, mother, father), rather than more distant blood relatives (e.g. cousin, nephew), because the closer the blood relationship the greater the genetic similarity. This theory's message should be very clear: altruistic acts will be directed towards those that share a genetic history, with the probability of performing altruistic acts decreasing as the genetic similarity decreases. Consequently, kin selection theory clearly predicts that altruistic behaviour should be most apparent amongst close relatives than among distant relatives or non-relatives. So is this prediction supported? It would seem that it is as studies carried out to test it are most often consistent with the prediction.

Perhaps one of the best studies to test kin selection theory's prediction is Sherman's (1977) study of a Belding's ground squirrel colony. As we have already seen (p. 16), when a predator appears the first squirrel to see it invariably gives an alarm call. However, it must be noted that they do not always give an alarm call (to others), so consequently alarm calls are not a simple innate response to a predator and must therefore involve a more complex response.

Sherman observed the squirrels over several generations, marking them with blotches of coloured dye to enable him to readily and reliably identify each individual. Within this colony young males left the area before they were one year old, and Sherman thus determined that all of the adult males present in the colony had been born elsewhere. Hence in this colony the males over one year old were not related to the females, or to any squirrels less than a year old that were not their offspring. On the other hand, females tended to stay in the colony they were born into; therefore many had relatives living in the immediate vicinity of their burrows, but also had other unrelated females living in the 'neighbourhood'. Consequently, the females in the colony were related to far more squirrels in the colony than the males were. As kin selection theory would predict, Sherman found that, on spotting a predator, females (having more relatives in the area than males) gave far more alarm calls than the males did. 'Aha,' you may cry, 'but this could simply be a matter of sex differences, with females generally being more altruistic than males.' However, Sherman also observed that the females that had relatives living in close proximity were far more likely to give an alarm call than those females that did not have relatives living in close vicinity. This finding is also supportive of kin selection theory's prediction because such altruism would be directed more at close relatives than distant relatives or non-relatives.

Another study that offers support for the kin selection theory is that of Hoogland (1983), who studied black-tailed prairie dogs. These dogs live in social groups, called coteries, which typically consist of one adult male and three-to-four adult females and their offspring. Young females remain in the coterie they were born into throughout their lives, but young males leave before they are two years old and disperse to join other coteries. Therefore all of the females and males within a coterie, aged 2 years or less, are close genetic relatives while males 2 years or older are not. If kin selection theory's prediction is correct then related dogs should exhibit greater altruistic behaviour to each other than non-related dogs. Like Belding's ground squirrel, the black-tailed prairie dog also emits alarm calls when a predator is spotted and it is this that (for Hoogland) constitutes altruistic behaviour. Hoogland presented the prairie dogs with a 'dummy' of a natural predator, a badger. Hoogland did this for two reasons. It enabled him to gain more data more quickly than if he had waited for a real natural predator to enter the prairie dogs' territory. And two, it allowed him to control for the proximity of the predator to the prairie dogs. Hoogland carried out over 700 experiments to establish whether relatives were more likely to be warned of approaching predators than non-relatives. He found that significantly more alarm calling occurred when 2–3 close relatives were in the coterie than when no close relatives were in the coterie.

An evaluation of kin selection theory

These studies of altruism, and many more, appear to be consistent with kin selection theory in that much of the altruism seen in nature does seem to occur more frequently between closely related individuals. Nevertheless, research has also shown that unrelated individuals also exhibit altruism, therefore undermining the kin selection theory. For example, Faaberg and Patterson (1981) observed that unrelated male Galapagos hawks frequently share a mate, copulating with her equally often, and that both put the same effort into rearing the subsequent offspring. Packer (1977) observed that there is fierce competition for females that are receptive to mating in olive baboons (*Papio anubis*). Other male baboons will go to great lengths to steal a female from a male baboon defending a receptive female that he has claimed. Packer observed that unrelated male olive baboons often form pairs to mate with receptive females, as it appears that pairs are much more successful at defending a female than is a single baboon. Therefore kin selection is not a complete explanation of altruism, as it can only explain altruism when altruist and recipient are genetically related. An explanation for altruism in non-relatives is therefore required.

Kin selection theory requires an individual to recognise that another individual *is* kin and how the individual is related to them. Hamilton's explanation of how individuals recognise kin and non-kin is also a shortcoming of the kin selection theory. Hamilton's explanation claims that there may be 'recognition alleles' (an allele refers to one or more different forms of a given gene) that enable animals to recognise these alleles in others and to behave altruistically towards them. This is a rather complex explanation, but it can be clarified by referring to Richard Dawkins' explanation (he refers to it as the 'green beard effect'). Dawkins states that if a gene enabled an individual to have both a green beard and a tendency to behave altruistically towards others with a green beard, it would be favoured by evolution. While Dawkins' explanation of how Hamilton claims that animals recognise kin is rather amusing it is theoretically improbable that a rather psychological characteristic (recognising someone) is genetically determined. So how do individuals recognise kin?

Explanations of kin recognition

Fortunately, a number of alternative explanations have been forwarded that are much more probable than Hamilton's – such as recognition by location, association mechanism and phenotype matching.

Kin recognition by location

This explanation claims that animals recognise kin by location and not by physical appearance, therefore it works on the basic principle of 'treat anyone in a specific location (e.g. territory, nest) as kin'. This may lead to behaving inappropriately altruistically to non-kin; for example, birds that feed a cuckoo's offspring after the cuckoo has placed egg(s) in an unrelated bird's nest. However, this strategy will only be successful for animals that remain in the same location; it would not be a successful strategy for those animals that do not remain in the same area.

Kin recognition by association

This explanation proposes that individuals learn to recognise each other because they have associated with each other from birth. More basically, it states that individuals adhere to the principle of 'those you grow up with are kin'. Konrad Lorenz, one of the first people to propose the association mechanism explanation, referred to it as 'imprinting'. Imprinting refers to a form of restricted learning that takes place within a relatively short time-span, and which is rather permanent (it cannot be altered). A classic example of association mechanism (or imprinting) is Lorenz's findings that goslings follow the first discernible moving object that they see after they hatch. Fortunately, this is usually their mother, and consequently would result in them following the thing that will increase the probability that they will survive and reproduce. Holmes and Sherman's (1982) experimental research can offer support for this explanation. They reared ground squirrels in one of four groups: siblings reared together (1) or siblings reared apart (2), and non-siblings reared together (3) or reared apart (4). The researchers found that when they later placed all these squirrels together those reared together (i.e. groups 1 and 3) rarely fought, irrespective of genetic relatedness. Consequently, it appears that the squirrels learned that those they are raised with are seen as kin and so behave less aggressively towards them than to those they have not been reared with. However, Holmes and Sherman also found that of the squirrels reared apart the genetically related squirrels were less aggressive towards each other than were the non-genetically related squirrels.

Kin recognition by phenotype matching

Recognition by phenotype matching occurs when individuals recognise kin and non-kin by comparing phenotypes (e.g. physical or behavioural characteristics) to establish whether they reflect genotype similarity. Consequently phenotype matching simply involves matching two individuals' physical or behavioural characteristics, often for purposes of kin recognition. For example, to determine if someone is related to you, you might compare their characteristics to your memory of what your relatives are like, or you might use yourself as a reference (self-referent phenotype matching) rather than your close relatives. The idea that animals can distinguish unfamiliar kin from unrelated strangers by knowing something about themselves or relatives, such as their visual image, their voice or their own smell, has been debated for more than thirty years. It is only recently, though, that relatively strong evidence has been gained to support this explanation of how animals recognise kin. Self-referent phenotype matching has long been suspected, but until the recent laboratory experiment by Mateo and Johnston (2000), who studied this phenomenon in golden hamsters (*Mesocricetus auratus*), had not been seen. This study has shown that golden hamsters use their own scent to distinguish unrelated hamsters from their biological siblings.

Mateo and Johnston separated newborn laboratory hamsters from their mothers and siblings before their odour-sensing capabilities had developed, and placed them with unrelated mothers and unrelated young hamsters. Consequently, being raised among strangers, the hamsters supposedly had no kin smell cues except their own. Seven weeks later, when the young females were sexually mature and their odour-sensing capabilities were at their best, the researchers presented the separated-at-birth hamsters with a choice of flank-gland scents (NB hamster smells come from scent glands on their flanks, referred to as flank glands). The flank-gland scents were from a variety of other hamsters consisting of unrelated and closely related kin, and familiar and unknown hamsters. The researchers tested the females at a time in their reproductive cycles when they would be very likely to be selecting a mate, and are most interested in odours. Mateo and Johnston reasoned that if the hamsters could recognise kin by flank-gland scent they would avoid male hamsters that were related because this is far less likely to result in viable offspring. Therefore if these females are to produce viable offspring then it is vital for them to be able to recognise their unfamiliar siblings so they can avoid mating with them. It was found that the separated-at-birth hamsters consistently selected unrelated mates and not unfamiliar biological siblings or unrelated foster siblings, therefore supporting the phenotype matching as an explanation for recognising kin.

Conclusion on kin selection theory

While the credibility of kin selection theory is weakened by Hamilton's explanation of kin recognition this is not a real problem because there are other appropriate alternative explanations of kin recognition. However, research into this is in its infancy, so it is too early to conclude which alternative is the better explanation of how animals recognise kin, although the most promising at present appears to be phenotype matching.

Reciprocal altruism theory (Trivers, 1971)

Reciprocal altruism is an arrangement whereby one individual helps another at some risk to themselves, and does so because they assume that the act will be reciprocated (returned) at some later time. Therefore it differs from kin selection in that it can explain altruistic behaviour among non-relatives. Reciprocal altruism is consequently a major alternative to kin selection, involving an appealing notion that reciprocity is the reason for the existence of altruism without the need to make any reference to or assumptions about other animals' genetic relatedness (indeed reciprocal altruism could even operate between members of different species). If an animal performs an altruistic act for another but has this act reciprocated at a later time then the cost is outweighed by the benefit of receiving altruism in return. Therefore, while behaving altruistically may decrease the probability that an animal will survive, the later reciprocal altruism will increase the probability that it will survive. Consequently, the existence of altruism may, overall, be more beneficial to survival than if it did not exist.

Trivers' reciprocal altruism theory is therefore expressing a crude biological version of the claim that altruism exists because animals are able to function more effectively when they work together than when they work alone. Put very simply it is a case of 'you scratch my back and I'll scratch yours'.

The implications raised by this theory are that in order for reciprocal altruism to be a viable system then, as a practical matter, three conditions must exist:

1 To enable reciprocity to occur animals must be able to recognise individuals.
2 Individuals must not be able to get away with failing to reciprocate (therefore cheat) without the original altruist being able to punish the cheat effectively – for example, by ostracising it from the group.
3 A high probability that the altruist's and recipient's situations will be reversed so that the recipient of the altruistic act will be able to reciprocate the act to the altruist in the future.

These conditions suggest that reciprocity is most likely to evolve among intelligent closely integrated species of animal in which the opportunities for reciprocity and recognition of individuals would be at their greatest.

Empirical support for reciprocal altruism

There are a number of instances of what appears to be reciprocal altruism.

As we have already seen when considering kin selection theory, Packer (1977) observed that unrelated male olive baboons 'team up' to increase the likelihood that one of them will mate with a receptive female. Therefore the non-mating male is acting altruistically towards the other male of the pair as he is incurring great potential costs in defending the female: he is at risk of being attacked yet he is receiving no benefits for his effort (cost to altruist). However, it was found that the altruist does ultimately benefit, because Packer also observed that when another receptive female becomes available the same males tend to pair up again. This time it is the altruist that mates with the receptive female, while the beneficiary of the initial altruistic behaviour guards the female and gains no benefits for his effort. Therefore – in terms of Trivers' claim that in order for altruism to evolve benefit from reciprocation must outweigh the cost of the initial altruistic act – the cost of guarding a female while the other baboon in the pair mates with her is outweighed by the benefit of increasing the probability that the altruist will successfully mate with a female. Consequently, such altruistic behaviour is favoured because male baboons acting in pairs are far more likely to achieve successful mating with receptive females than are single males.

Wilkinson (1984) observed one of the most astounding examples of reciprocal altruism in a roost of vampire bats (*Desmodus rotundus*). Vampire bats can only survive for around 48 hours without food. Wilkinson found that if a bat has been unsuccessful at foraging for blood it returns to the roost to beg food from other bats, upon which a donor regurgitates blood for the hungry bat to drink. Hence the donor bat is behaving altruistically towards the hungry bat because it is giving away food that it has spent a great deal of energy gaining and it may not gain enough food on subsequent foraging trips to make up the loss. Wilkinson studied kin relationships in the roost and found that bats only behaved altruistically towards either close relatives or unrelated individuals that regularly roosted with them. Quite clearly if a donor bat is a relative of the recipient of their donation then kin selection theory can explain why this occurs, although it can't explain why this occurs in unrelated bats. Reciprocal altruism theory can. The cost of a well-fed bat donating a little blood to another is small, but the cost is outweighed by the fact that it may ultimately benefit. This could be because the bat who received help will be able to go out foraging another day and return the favour when the altruist comes back from an unsuccessful foraging trip.

Evaluation of reciprocal altruism theory

As reciprocal altruism requires certain conditions to be viable (see p. 25) it is probably much rarer in the real world than kin-selected altruism, though it is a theoretical possibility – as seems to be clearly demonstrated in the examples above. Nevertheless, the greatest problem for reciprocal altruism is the potential for cheating – that is, taking the help offered but not returning the favour. At the individual level cheating would be a viable strategy as it enables an individual to increase the probability that it will survive and reproduce, but at no cost. Simultaneously, cheating would cause the altruist to lose fitness because the costs associated with the altruistic act are not compensated by later reciprocation. Nevertheless, cheating may only result in short-term benefits and in the long term may result in a detrimental effect on the animal's survival and reproductive success. This is because reciprocity is most likely to evolve among intelligent closely harmonised social species where recognition of individuals would be at its greatest. Consequently, in such species a cheat will eventually be recognised and can be excluded from future transactions and may even be prevented from remaining in the group; this, in turn, might be detrimental to the cheater's survival and consequent reproductive success. Nevertheless, the possibility of cheats being detected and punished still poses a problem because this, in turn, may lead to natural selection of greater skilfulness among cheaters to try to avoid detection. Therefore because of these problems the efficiency of reciprocity as an explanation for the evolution of altruism in animals is not well understood. At present, however, of all species it is probably most appropriate for explaining altruism in humans (*Homo sapiens*).

Manipulated altruism (or social parasitism)

As we have seen earlier, natural selection normally results in animals behaving in ways that support their own selfish interests. Even when natural selection favours altruism it is only in terms of some general form of selfishness – for example, having the altruism reciprocated or passing ones genes into the next generation by helping a relative's reproductive success. Manipulated altruism theory is a recent proposal (1989) that claims that animals have a series of learned and innate behaviours that normally increase the probability that they will survive, reproduce and rear viable offspring. However, such behaviours are open to being exploited by others; this is how manipulated altruism is said to occur. In manipulated altruism the recipient of help exploits the helper's behaviours and gains the help without the helper's knowledge.

Probably the best way to clarify manipulated altruism is by using an example. The European cuckoo (*Cuculus canorus*) exploits a parental bird's normal behaviours of keeping eggs warm until they hatch and then putting food into a gaping chick's mouth until it is able to get food for itself. It exploits the parental bird's behaviour by destroying one of the host bird's (parental bird that the cuckoo exploits) eggs and replacing it with one of its own. The host bird keeps the cuckoo's planted egg warm until it hatches with its own eggs and then puts food into the newly hatched cuckoo's gaping mouth. Therefore the host bird raises the cuckoo's offspring – sometimes even when the cuckoo's offspring is almost too large for the host bird's nest and much bigger than the host bird. This is a clear case of a bird exploiting the host bird's behaviour in order to make life and reproduction easier on itself.

Empirical support for manipulated altruism

Examples of manipulated altruism are particularly common in fish, birds and insects, and many such instances have been observed and reported. For example, Hölldobler (1971) found that the larvae of the rove beetle (*Atemeles*) gains entrance to the nest of its host *Myrmica* ants by mimicking the ants' chemical communication system. The beetle then releases a secretion from its appeasement gland, which suppresses the ants' aggressive behaviour towards the intruder. The beetle then releases a secretion from its adoption gland that then stimulates the ants to carry the beetle into the nest where the beetle then lays its eggs. The beetle's maturing larvae have rows of glands that secrete a substance that stimulates the ants to regurgitate food for it. Consequently, the ant is unwittingly behaving highly altruistically to the rove beetle by escorting it to its nest and tending its offspring.

Wickler (1968) found that sabre-toothed blenny fish (*Aspidontus*) mimic the appearance of cleaner fish. Cleaner fish are small fish that remove parasites, scales and mucous from the external surface of larger fish (referred to as 'clients'), and therefore keep the client healthy. The reason that the sabre-toothed blenny mimics the cleaner fish is to ensure that the client fish will allow it to approach it without eating it. However, unlike the helpful cleaner fish, the mimicking sabre-toothed blenny approaches the client fish with the pretence of cleaning it, but instead takes a chunk of flesh from the client fish, consequently gaining a free meal at its expense. Therefore the sabre-toothed blenny fish is exploiting the client fish's response to cleaner fish, as by mimicking the cleaner fish it causes the client fish to respond to it as if it were a cleaner fish.

Evaluation of manipulated altruism

It appears that this explanation could explain why this type of altruism would be selected: it increases the probability that such freeloaders will survive and successfully reproduce, while at the same time decreasing the unwitting helper's fitness. Such behaviour is in keeping with Darwin's notion of the survival of the fittest and therefore has gone a long way to solving the paradox of this type of altruism at least.

Conclusion on evolutionary explanations of altruism

Probably the most feasible evolutionary explanation of altruism is the kin selection theory, though it does not explain the mechanisms of the evolution of altruism in non-related animals or different species adequately. It also fails to explain adequately how animals recognise kin; hence it is not a complete explanation. Nevertheless, the theory of reciprocal altruism can explain the mechanisms of the evolution of altruism in related and non-related animals (or different species). It does not, however, explain why altruism appears to be much more apparent in related animals than it is in unrelated animals. This failure is problematic because it suggests that altruism must be more complex than simple reciprocity. Manipulated altruism has basically solved the paradox – at least for this type of altruistic behaviour. Nevertheless some researchers have recently questioned whether altruism really exists in the animal kingdom (Clutton-Brock *et al.*, 1999).

Until recently many scientists had long believed that individual meerkats (*Suricata suricatta*) act selflessly when they act as lookout, taking turns to watch out for predators while the others in their group forage for insects. When a sentinel (guarding) meerkat spies a predator it yelps a warning call and the entire group then darts for cover in the nearest burrows. Sentinels not only appeared to sacrifice the chance to feed in order to guard the safety of the group, but scientists also believed that they placed themselves at higher risk by exposing themselves on high perches and drawing attention to their location with the alarm call.

Recently, however, some scientists, most notably Clutton-Brock and his colleagues, have questioned the altruistic interpretation of these sentinels.

After more than 2,000 hours of observing five packs of meerkats, Clutton-Brock and his research group (1999) reported that they did not see a single sentinel attacked or killed by a predator. This led them to conclude that sentinel meerkats are actually looking out for their own skins. The researchers came to this conclusion because not only were these individuals the first to see the predators, they were also the first ones to get below ground. This behaviour cannot be explained by kin selection, as Clutton-Brock *et al.* found that every meerkat in a group, whether relatives or not, take turns standing guard. Moreover, they learned that a meerkat was only likely to stand guard if it had already eaten enough to fill its belly.

Clutton-Brock *et al.*'s meerkat study is only the latest in a string of new cases that claim to disprove the existence of animal altruism. Another example is one involving the raven (*Corvus corax*), thought to be behaving altruistically when calling to their peers on finding a carcass (Heinrich and Marzluff, 1995). Researchers previously interpreted such behaviour as altruistic, because by alerting their peers to their find it meant they would receive less food. It has now been pointed out that ravens only call their peers when the carcass they have found is in another raven group's territory. By calling their peers, therefore, the individual is 'beefing up' its defence against rival birds and is increasing the probability that it will get some of the carcass – a highly unlikely prospect if it tried to defend the carcass as an individual. Another example is the supposedly altruistic behaviour in swallows (Brown *et al.*, 1991), whereby an individual swallow gives a call to other swallows on finding a swarm of insects. While it was previously thought that these swallows were behaving altruistically in sharing their find, more recent research has shown that swallows are more effective at catching insects in a swarm when doing so as a group than they are as individuals. Thus the caller birds are simply selfishly alerting the other birds to improve their own chances of gaining a meal.

All of these studies clearly show that many animals seem to act in their own self-interest and not, as was previously thought, selflessly. Therefore interpreting animals as behaving altruistically may, in the future, turn out to be due to anthropomorphic researchers. If this does turn out to be the case then altruism will no longer be a paradox for

Darwin's theory of evolution, because it will have been shown that it does not exist in the animal kingdom. At present, though, it still remains a paradox.

Evolutionary explanations of territoriality

Attempts have also been made to offer a number of evolutionary explanations for territorial behaviour in animals.

An introduction to territorial behaviour

Territoriality (territorial behaviour) refers to the tendency of animals to defend a particular area – usually against members of the same species. Howard (1920) was the first to elaborate the concept of territoriality, with particular reference to birds; these still remain the most studied.

Research has shown that animals defend their territories by way of a series of specialised behaviour patterns. Characteristically there are three tiers to territorial defence. The first tier of territorial defence behaviour is to give a long-distance signal in the form of scent markers (urine, faeces or secretions from a special scent gland) or by specific warning vocalisations; both act to keep intruders away. Krebs *et al.*'s (1978) study clearly shows the effectiveness of territorial defence signals. The study involved removing great tits from their territories and placing loudspeakers that broadcast the great tit song in half of these now-undefended territories. It was found that the broadcast of the song alone kept intruders at bay, but intruders quickly invaded territories where no such song was broadcast. The second tier of territorial defence behaviour, should an intruder fail to be deterred by the first tier (signalling), is generally a warning display of some sort. For example, a bird may fluff its feathers up to appear larger and more threatening; a wolf may bare its teeth and a lion may roar. The third tier, should the display fail to deter a persistent intruder, will be to fight the intruder off.

As animals often invest substantial resources in defence of their territory evolutionary explanations state that such behaviour will only be adaptive if in the long run the benefits gained from doing so exceed the costs of defence. Evolutionary explanations of territoriality suggest that it is adaptive when two major requirements are met:

1 There must be competition among individuals for territories, otherwise there is no need for defence.

2 The territory must be economically defensible; that is, the benefits of keeping the territory should not be outweighed by the costs of defending it.

When both of these conditions are met then the benefits are sufficient to compensate the costs of territorial defence, therefore this type of behaviour will be naturally selected.

Based on the assumption that these two requirements are met a number of attempts to explain why territoriality is adaptive have been put forward. The three that will be covered here are:

- Explanation of territorial behaviour as a means of gaining an adequate food source.
- Explanation of territorial behaviour as a means of gaining a satisfactory mate.
- Game theory as an evolutionary explanation for territorial behaviour.

Explanation of territorial behaviour as a means of gaining an adequate food source

The English zoologist Wynne-Edwards (1962) observed that the size of the territory in a given species varied from year to year – if food was plentiful territories were small in comparison to when food was scarce. Based on this observation he proposed that maintaining territories is part of natural selection because it ensures that animals gain an adequate food supply for their own survival and for any offspring produced. This explanation is thought to be too simplistic to be able to explain territorial behaviour, however, as it appears that this type of behaviour is much more complex than simply trying to ensure an adequate supply of food.

Explanation of territorial behaviour as a means of gaining an adequate mate

More traditional explanations claim that territoriality evolved because it enhanced an individual's probability of gaining an adequate mate.

This is thought to be so because holding and maintaining the territory demonstrated the individual's fitness, as it had, for example, competed with others, or had obtained and defended territory successfully. Such territory would therefore enable access to other resources such as food and water. Consequently, such an animal would advertise its fitness to a potential mate as having the characteristics necessary to obtain and defend a territory successfully, and should therefore possess adaptive genes and pass these characteristics on to the next generation. However, it has since been realised that territorial behaviour is much more complex than advocates of this explanation would have us believe. For example, how does obtaining and holding territory ensure that the individual will actually select a mate that will be fertile and produce viable offspring? If the individual chooses a mate that is not fertile then it reduces the fitness of the holder of the territory.

Game theory as an evolutionary explanation for territorial behaviour

Probably the most viable evolutionary explanation to date is Maynard-Smith's (1974) game theory. In order to enable a critical understanding of this theory it is useful to consider how game theory works and the related terminology involved before the theory is examined in more detail.

An introduction to game theory

Game theory proposes that different strategies will be used when competing for limited resources – in this case territory, because the valuable resources in the territory enable the holder to have access to these. Strategies are simply possible courses of action that are available to an animal (i.e. in its repertoire) and that it could engage in. For example, one animal's strategy may be to fight to defend its territory whereas another may choose to retreat and give up the territory. A more complex strategy may be to fight to defend the territory until it can be gauged how strong the challenger is – if stronger than you retreat, if weaker fight on. Therefore strategies will be selected because they increase the animal's fitness more than any other alternative strategies. Hence they offer an optimal (ideal) solution and are called **evolutionary stable strategies** (ESS).

An ESS is a strategy which, if most members of a population adopt it, cannot be replaced by an alternative strategy because, of all possible strategies, it has proved to be the most successful and therefore has been naturally selected. To make this clear we will consider the example of reciprocal altruism as one strategy and 'sponging' (i.e. accepting help but not returning the favour) as an alternative strategy, and consider how an ESS can evolve from these. (NB the following example can also serve to show how group selection occurs.)

Consider a population in which reciprocal altruism has also evolved individuals that are cheaters. Initially cheaters will have an advantage over helpers because they will enjoy all of the benefits of the altruistic system without incurring any of the costs; therefore cheaters will be selected, making cheaters initially fitter than helpers. However, in the long term this will decrease the cheaters' fitness because it will result in an increase in cheaters in the population and a decrease in helpers so that there will not be enough helpers to sustain the cheaters. Indeed, if the cheaters carry on exploiting the helpers and further reducing numbers this behaviour is no longer adaptive (just the opposite in fact) as cheaters are only able to use this strategy when there are helpers to exploit. This decline in available helpers, together with the advantage that the remaining helpers will get from helping one another, will then outweigh the advantage of being exploited and the helpers will start to make a comeback. However, the helpers' comeback will be held in check because their recovery provides an advantage for the cheaters because potential helpers have now increased. Nevertheless, if the cheaters then over-exploit the helpers again these latter will decrease and the cheaters will be faced with the same problem – a decrease in their fitness. Eventually, due to this dependency, the ratio of helpers and cheaters will become balanced to ensure that the remaining reproductive success is the best under that given set of circumstances. Consequently the ratio of cheaters to helpers has evolved into an ESS because any shift away from it results in decreasing success for both animals.

In very simple terms then, if humans were to eat all available food before animals and plants had time to reproduce it would be detrimental to humans, animals and plants. And while this may seem like a good strategy when food is plentiful it would result in all three (humans, animals and plants) eventually becoming extinct. Thus an ESS would be to balance humans' consumption of these with the reproduction rate of animals and plants (and human for that matter) so that there will always be a constant supply; this would be an ESS.

According to Maynard-Smith the process of natural selection is what has led to the evolution of territoriality, as it is, he claims, an evolutionary stable strategy (ESS)

In game theory, the term 'game' means a particular sort of conflict in which individuals or groups (known as players) participate – in this case trying to obtain and/or defend territory. In order to establish how an EES evolves game theory goes through a series of stages to work out, mathematically, what strategies might be available and the possible consequences of adopting the strategies. Game theory's mathematical calculation of strategies and consequences is viewed very much like a game, with the 'rules' of the game consisting of the following:

1 The conditions under which the game begins.
2 The possible legal 'moves' at each stage of play.
3 The total number of moves constituting the entirety of the game.
4 The terms of the outcome at the end of play.

However, it must be stressed that game theory does not suggest that evolutionary progress is the same when a theorist constructs a game theory. Instead the game is used as a means of mathematically calculating plausible strategies and consequences of adopting the strategies.

When a theorist constructs a game theory s/he compiles a list of plausible strategies that the theorist believes an animal might feasibly use. The next step involves producing a definition of costs and benefits (measured in terms of fitness) that will be allocated when individuals playing various plausible strategies (created in the first stage) interact with each other. Then, based on the mathematics of game theory, there is a formal mathematical analysis to establish which strategy, if any, would be an ESS. The theorist then observes the animal behaviour in its natural environment to see if it actually fits what the formal mathematical analysis predicted.

Applying game theory

Maynard-Smith (1974) first applied game theory in a relatively simple form, involving only two strategies, which he called 'hawk' and 'dove'. It should again be stressed that the theory does not refer to real hawks and doves but simply a specific strategy an animal could use. The terms are borrowed from military metaphors which refer to humans.

The hawk strategy is very aggressive, always fighting for some resource and involving the following rules:

- Fights between hawks are fierce affairs with the loser being the one who first sustains injury, upon which the winner takes sole possession of the territory.
- Although hawks that lose a contest are injured, the rules of the game require that they do not die and in fact are fully recovered before the next expected contest.
- For simplicity, it is assumed that all hawks are equal in fighting ability; that is, each hawk has a 50 per cent chance of winning a hawk–hawk conflict. Another way of saying this is that hawk versus hawk contests are symmetrical.

The dove strategy involves never fighting for a resource. Instead, it displays non-aggressive behaviour in any conflict and if it is attacked it immediately withdraws before it gets injured:

- In any conflict situation, a dove will always lose the resource to a hawk, but it never gets hurt (i.e. it never sustains a decrease in fitness) when confronting a hawk; consequently the interactions are neutral with respect to the dove's fitness.
- Doves do not display for very long against hawks, therefore after starting their displays they immediately recognise that their opponent is a hawk and withdraw without paying a meaningful display cost.
- If a dove meets a dove there will be a period of displaying with some cost (time, energy for display) but no injury. It is assumed that all doves are equally good at displaying and will adopt a strategy of waiting for a random time period. Therefore when two doves face off, each has a 50 per cent chance of winning.
- Both doves will pay essentially the same display cost in any contest. The winner is the individual willing to pay more. However, note that the winner stops displaying at essentially the same time as the loser withdraws.

There are also two other important assumptions in the application of game theory:

- It assumes that the attacking animal (the one that either starts first to physically attack or to display) has no knowledge of the strategy that its opponent will play.
- It assumes that these interactions increase or decrease the animal's fitness from some baseline fitness. Put another way, these interactions simply modify an animal's fitness up or down. (NB winning a contest does create fitness.) This assumption is associated with the custom that injuries and display costs will be assigned negative scores. Losing animals, however, does not mean that animals will have negative fitness.

While the hawk and dove strategies are not meant to be fully representative of the strategies of real animals, they are meant to represent the essence of the biological problem of survival and allow a prediction to be made about which strategy natural selection will favour in a given situation. Put more basically, game theory answers the question as to why natural selection does not cause a population that consists of animals just using the hawk strategy or just using the dove strategy to evolve. It gains the answer to this question by calculating the effect of an animal using the dove strategy or the hawk strategy on the animal's fitness – that is, fitness in terms of an increase (benefits) or a decrease (costs) in the number of offspring an individual would produce. (Maynard-Smith calls these costs and benefits 'pay-offs'.) It then allows an estimate as to which strategy (or combination of strategies), if any, natural selection will favour in a given situation. Maynard-Smith therefore began his application of game theory with the creation of a list of plausible hawk and dove strategies. He then estimated all of the possible pay-offs to each strategy by giving numerical values to all possible outcomes, and applying a definition of costs and benefits that could be allocated when individuals, playing various plausible strategies (created in the first stage), interact with each other. For example, in the straightforward hawk–dove game there are two costs: the cost of serious injury (called C), which Maynard-Smith allocated a numerical value of 100; and the time cost of a prolonged dispute in terms of the amount of time and energy used (called T), which Maynard-Smith allocated a numerical value of 10. However, the benefit that the winner would gain is increased fitness (called V), which Maynard-Smith allocated a numerical value of 50.

Then, based on the mathematical principles of game theory, Maynard-Smith applied a formal mathematical analysis to establish which strategy, if any, would be an ESS. Thus, if a dove meets a dove, either is equally likely to back down in a conflict over territory. However, doves are also likely to have a lengthy dispute using valuable energy, therefore slightly reducing their fitness; so the calculation would be V (50) minus T (10) = 40 divided by 2 (because either have an equal chance of 'winning' the territory). Consequently this strategy has a fitness value of 20. However, if a hawk meets a hawk then, while each has an equal chance of 'winning' the territory, there is also equal chance that they will sustain serious injury and thus greatly reduce their fitness. So the calculation would be V (50) minus C (100) = minus 50 divided by 2, consequentially giving this strategy a fitness value of minus 25. This suggests that dove strategy is the superior of the two, but (obviously) it is not as simple as this. This is because it depends on how many doves and hawks are in a population at any given time and how many alternative strategies there are. Initially Maynard-Smith only used two strategies – hawk and dove – to simplify the aim of the theory and make this much clearer.

Maynard-Smith stated that both types of strategy generally confer some advantages to the individual who uses them, but also that both also incur costs. Nevertheless, if there is a balance between the costs and benefits for both hawk and dove strategy then it will result in an evolutionary stable strategy because neither hawk nor dove strategy *always* has an advantage over the other.

To make it clear why neither hawk nor dove strategy *always* has an advantage over the other, and why a balance between hawk and dove strategies would always be reverted to (i.e. an EES), we can look at both strategies in the same way as we considered helpers and cheaters.

Consider a situation that arose where there were more animals using the hawk strategy than the dove strategy; the unrestrained aggression of the hawk strategy would greatly reduce the survival (and hence reproducing) of those using this strategy. As a consequence of this more animals would begin using the dove strategy because it has become more adaptive to do so (i.e. it has reduced the animal's fitness as it has reduced the probability that it will survive and reproduce). Therefore there would now be fewer animals using the hawk strategy because it has become less adaptive.

Now that more animals are adopting the dove strategy when there is a challenge for valuable territory both will back down and neither will obtain or retain it; consequently this strategy will reduce the fitness of those animals using it. However, those who now adopt the hawk strategy can challenge animals using the dove strategy and easily win the territory. Thus the hawk strategy will now be the more adaptive strategy as it will increase an animal's fitness in this situation. Nevertheless, if those using the hawk strategy increase, outnumbering those using the dove strategy, we are back to the scenario at the beginning of this example. As a result of this the unrestrained aggression of the hawk strategy would greatly reduce the number of surviving (and hence reproducing) hawks. Consequently, the whole process would begin again. In sum, it would *always revert back to a balance between dove and hawk strategy!*

The hawk–dove game can be likened to the old game of stone, paper and scissors whereby players use one of three strategies to try to win the game: (1) stone strategy by holding out a clenched fist; (2) paper strategy by holding out the flattened palm of the hand; (3) scissors

Table 2.1 Hawk and dove strategies		
Strategy used by player 1	*Strategy used by player 2*	*Consequences of strategy*
Hawk	Hawk	Both have an equal chance of sustaining serious injury, thus greatly reducing their fitness
Hawk	Dove	Player 1 will win
Dove	Hawk	Player 2 will win
Dove	Dove	Either is equally likely to back down in a conflict over territory

strategy by forming the index and second finger into a scissors-shape. In this game the stone beats scissors, paper beats stone and scissors beat paper. This game can also show why it would be disadvantageous not to adopt a variety of strategies. Consider what would happen if most of the players decided to adopt the stone strategy consistently; very quickly they would be knocked out of the game by paper strategists. This would leave only paper and scissors strategists in the game and if they failed to adopt a change of strategies the game would end very quickly because scissors strategists would quickly knock the paper strategists out the game. Therefore, for the game to continue effectively, a variety of strategies must be adopted.

Evaluation of game theory

In order to evaluate game theory it just remains to be established whether behaviour observed in nature actually fits what game theory predicts. Research has shown that the fit between predictions made by game theory and animal behaviour observed in the natural environment is often supportive. For example, game theory makes three predictions about territorial behaviour:

1 If animal x 'owns' the territory then when an intruder – animal y – makes a stake for the territory animal x will always adopt a hawk strategy and animal y will always adopt a dove strategy. Hence animal x will always keep its territory.
2 If the reverse situation exists (that is, animal y 'owns' the territory and animal x is the intruder) then animal y will always keep its territory.
3 If an animal believes it 'owns' the territory it will always use the hawk strategy and fight to retain ownership. When animals x and y both believe they own the territory they will adopt the hawk strategy, resulting in a long and escalated fight with a high probability of serious injury.

Davies (1978) offers support that the above predictions do appear to fit observations in the real world. He showed that speckled wood butterflies appear to conform to these predictions and, therefore, show an EES. Davies found that when the first butterfly to settle in a temporary mating territory ('owner') is confronted by an intruder there is a brief and highly ritualised (organised and restrained) fight from which the intruder always withdraws and the owner retains the territory. However when he exchanged the butterflies so that the previous intruder was now the owner and the previous owner was now the intruder the new owner always retained the territory. Moreover, when Davies placed both butterflies in the territory at the same time, but placed a screen between them so that both believed they were the first there and then lifted the screen, it was found that both butterflies adopted the hawk strategy. This resulted in a long, escalated fight with neither butterfly willing to back down, consequently supporting the above three predictions made by game theory.

While there does appear to be evidence that confirms the predictions made by game theory there have been a number of objections aimed at it. For example, the fact that it is the theorist that decides what constitutes a plausible strategy or strategies for an animal, on the basis of what they believe the animal could do, is somewhat dubious. As is the theorist's decision about the 'pay-offs' of adopting a particular strategy, especially when we consider the enormous diversity in animal behaviour. However, one of the biggest criticisms of game theory is its total reliance on confirming examples from animal research to show its appropriateness; this places its validity under serious doubt. Any explanation that adopts a research technique whereby a logical mathematical argument is first drawn up, followed by finding examples of animal behaviour that fit the argument (confirmatory evidence), and then claims that such evidence proves that, in principle, the explanation is correct, is a very weak argument. This greatest weakness lies in the fact that such a technique is unable to tell us anything at all about the animals whose behaviour does not fit the explanation – a good theory should explain the entire phenomenon it is claiming to explain. Therefore game theory fails to offer a valid and full explanation of the evolution of territoriality.

Conclusion on evolutionary explanations of territorial behaviour

A number of evolutionary explanations of territoriality have been proposed, most of which are rather inadequate. The difficulty in providing an adequate evolutionary explanation of territoriality is that there are so many factors that could be potential reasons for territorial behaviour. At present, therefore, the theories forwarded appear to be too simplistic, and a great deal more research needs to be carried out before a satisfactory explanation is proposed.

Conclusion on evolutionary explanations of animal behaviour

It is claimed that evolution occurs due to natural selection choosing the 'fittest', but the question arises – the fittest what? For Darwin's theory of evolution the answer was clear that the fittest meant whatever qualities assisted an animal in its ability to survive and reproduce. Fitness includes qualities such as fast-running legs, keen eyes, abundant, high-quality milk, etc. Post-Darwinian evolutionists, however, claim that 'fittest' is a technical term used by mathematical geneticists to mean, 'whatever is favoured by natural selection'. This definition of fitness means that survival of the fittest is a tautology (i.e. it is stating the same thing but in a different way). This is because when we ask the question 'What is fitness?' the answer is 'Whatever is favoured by natural selection', and if we ask why natural selection has favoured a 'behaviour' the answer is 'because of its fitness'. Thus it is simply stating the same thing but in a different way and is therefore telling us little or nothing about the evolution of a behaviour in terms of its adaptability.

Furthermore, the idea, so convincingly argued by Darwin, that natural selection is the major principle by which evolutionary change occurs has been challenged by some scientists (e.g. Gould, 1989; Lloyd, 1988; Eldredge, 1995), and opinions now vary as to what the major principles of evolution in fact are. While many consider natural selection, at least in some form, to be the most important principle for evolution others claim different principles as the major determinants of evolution. For example, the most reasonable alternative to natural selection is genetic drift. This states that another force in evolutionary change is the accumulation of small, random, irrelevant changes that are not acted upon by natural selection. Another recently proposed alternative to natural selection is the application of the complexity theory to biological systems. This idea rests on the argument that matter has the tendency to self-organise into complicated systems, such as living organisms. At present little evidence is available to support this theory; however, it will eventually stand or fall on the evidence.

Finally, evolutionary explanations are but one type of explanation for animal behaviour and should not be used to the exclusion of alternative explanations. Preferably they should be used in conjunction with alternative explanations. Two such alternative explanations are the theory of co-evolution and learning theory.

The theory of co-evolution

Put very briefly this claims that evolution is not a simple one-way process involving individuals, who either adapt to environmental changes or fail to survive. Instead the theory of co-evolution claims that there is a two-way relationship between animal and environment in that the environment not only influences changes in animal behaviour but that animal behaviour also influences environmental changes. Indeed, as Rose (1983) so clearly points out, even an amoeba (a very basic organism in terms of evolution) changes the water it swims in as it consumes nutrients out the water and emits waste products into the water. Thus as a result the amoeba has changed the water and the change in water (environmental change) will now affect the amoeba. Therefore evolutionary forces are not simply the result of animals' adaptation to an **ecological niche** into which they successfully 'fitted'; rather, the animals and environment co-evolved as the environment is also forced to adapt to the animals' behaviour. Thus it would appear that co-evolution is much more multidimensional in its interpretation of animal behaviour than the more simplistic evolutionary explanations.

Learning theory

A very important alternative to evolutionary explanations of animal behaviour is learning theory. As the name suggests, this theory claims that most of animal behaviour is determined by learning and not, as evolutionary explanations suggest, by genetic inheritance. Classical and operant conditioning explanations of learning will be considered in depth in the next chapter.

Summary

In this chapter we have considered evolutionary attempts to explain behaviour in the terms of adaptation espoused by Darwin's theory of evolution. We have also seen that while evolution can explain some animal behaviour it is just one of many ways of explaining it. Indeed, there are a number of alternatives to evolutionary explanation, such as co-evolution and learning theory; consequently, because animal behaviour is highly varied and complex, evolution should not be used at the expense of these alternatives. Instead, a combination of all explanations of animal behaviour will probably result in a much richer understanding of animal behaviour.

Further reading

Dawkins, R. (1986) *The Blind Watchmaker*, New York: Norton. A very readable book that addresses many of the common misconceptions and false beliefs about Darwin's theory. Dawkins' style is clear and enjoyable and readily accessible to the A-level student.

Dawkins, R. (1997) 'Evolution', Microsoft Encarta 97 Encyclopaedia, World English Edition. This is a very clear and readable account of the history of evolutionary theory, evolutionary history, Darwinism, neo-Darwinism, the *Origin of Species*, the diversity of evolution, and the issues and arguments arising from explanations of evolution.

Manning, A. and Dawkins, M. S. (1992) *An Introduction to Animal Behaviour* (4th edn), Cambridge: Cambridge University Press. A good basic introductory text on animal behaviour.

3

Classical and operant conditioning

Introduction to conditioning theory

Evolution is not the only thing that determines an animal's behaviour – it is also determined by learning gained from an animal's experience in its environment. In psychology learning refers to a relatively permanent change in behaviour that occurs as the result of reinforcement. One type of learning is conditioning, of which there are two explanations: classical conditioning and operant conditioning. Both classical and operant conditioning attempt to explain exactly how an animal learns such new behaviours; thus they are learning theories. Furthermore, both classical conditioning theory and operant conditioning theory are based on **behaviourism**. Behaviourism is an approach in psychology that argues that the only appropriate subject matter for scientific psychological investigation is directly observable and measurable behaviour. Therefore behaviourists (those who take a behaviourism approach) claim that internal mental processes are not appropriate subject matter for scientific psychological investigation as they are not directly observable and measurable. Moreover, behaviourism regards any mental state as an **epiphenomenon** – that is a mental state is simply a state that happens to occur in the presence of observable behaviour but in fact plays no part in determining behaviour. To make this claim a little clearer consider the following: a fire may be lit to gain heat; however, when a fire occurs so does smoke but the smoke plays no part in making the fire produce heat – it is simply a useless by-product (i.e. an epiphenomenon). This is comparable to behaviourism's view of mental processes that occur when behaviour occurs, thus the belief that mental states or concepts play a part in determining behaviour is rejected.

The nature of classical conditioning and its role in the behaviour of animals

Every single organism has a number of innate *stimulus–response associations* – that is, connections that are 'wired in' the nervous system at birth – before any real opportunity for learning has taken place. For example a newborn infant will exhibit a blinking response if wind blows into its eyes and it will cry if it experiences pain; similarly, a hungry animal will salivate (produce saliva) when presented with food, will be sick if the food is 'bad', etc. These and many other responses do not have to be learned, nor is there any need to have conscious control over these reflexive responses. Animals, including humans, just do them automatically without the need for any conscious thought. Classical conditioning is based on these innate neurological connections, and classical conditioning theory claims that an animal learns new behaviours by way of learning an *association* between an involuntary *unconditional stimulus* (such as the smell of food when hungry) and another stimulus (i.e. something which can stimulate the senses).

To make association formation a little clearer consider the following. Let's suppose that we have acquired a new kitten and decided that we will feed the kitten at around 5.30 each evening. The first night we go to the cupboard where the cat food is kept, get a can out and place it on the worktop. We then open the utensil drawer and take out the can opener and proceed to open the cat food. When the smell of the food (unconditional stimulus) has been released from the can this will cause the hungry kitten to salivate (unconditional response) because this is an innate reflex – the kitten does not have to learn to salivate for it has been genetically programmed to do this when it is hungry and smells food. You repeat this kitten-feeding routine every evening for the next week. By the eighth day you find that the kitten is beginning to go to the place where its bowl is usually placed as soon as it hears or sees the can opener (associated stimulus). And a few days later you find that the kitten will salivate (unconditional stimulus) just at the sight or sound of the can opener (associated stimulus) when no cat food is presented. In fact this is exactly what happened when I first got my dog. She initially salivated at the smell of her food, then at the sight of the can opener; she then began to salivate at the sight of me getting a can out of the cupboard (associated stimulus) where I keep her food (and also cling film and kitchen foil). She also began to salivate when I went to the cupboard where I keep her food and took out cling film or kitchen foil. However, she quickly realised that she does not get food when I take out cling film or kitchen foil and learned not to salivate at the sight of me retrieving these, now only salivating when I take out a can of her food.

So how did the kitten and my dog learn to associate other stimuli with salivation? Probably the easiest way to understand how classical conditioning occurs is by starting with a basic example, introducing the terminology used, and then moving onto a more complex explanation involving applying this terminology.

An example of how classical conditioning can occur

Let us suppose that we wanted to teach your pet dog 'Fido' to whine loudly whenever your brother or sister played a particular record that you hate; a rather strange goal, but let's 'go with the flow'. According to classical conditioning theory you have to teach the dog to associate the whining response with the sound of the hated record; consequently, you have to find a stimulus that already causes the dog to whine. Therefore let's further suppose that you have noticed that whenever your next door neighbour's cat (unconditional stimulus) comes into your garden Fido whines (unconditional response) for all he is worth, but does not whine when the hated record is played. Having found this whine-inducing stimulus (the neighbour's cat) the next stage is to get Fido to learn to associate the whining (unconditional response) with the hated record. This can be done by placing the next door neighbour's cat in the garden where Fido can see it and then playing the hated record at about the same time, and repeating this 'pairing' of cat and record on a number of occasions. When a number of such 'pairings' have been presented to Fido you then simply play the record in the absence of the cat and – hey presto! – Fido whines for all he is worth. Fido has therefore formed an association between the cat (unconditional stimulus) and the hated record (conditional stimulus) in just the same way that the kitten and my dog formed an association between the smell of food and the can opener.

This is the essence of classical conditioning. You begin with two things that are already connected, in this example a cat (the unconditional stimulus) and whining (the unconditional response), and then add a third thing, in this case a specific record (the neutral stimulus), on a number of occasions. Eventually this third thing may become so strongly associated with one of the other things that it now has the power to produce the old behaviour (in this case whining). Fido now whines (as an association has been formed it becomes the conditional response) whenever he hears the hated record (as an association has been formed it becomes the conditional response). Yes, it really is that simple. What is a little trickier is learning and applying the terminology of classical conditioning theory. And while you have already been introduced to some of the terminology in the parentheses above, you may find these a little confusing at first. However, once you have the basic understanding of the principles of classical conditioning then understanding and remembering the terminology should be a much easier task.

In order to further understand the terminology associated with the principles of classical conditioning theory we can consider the historical development of classical conditioning and the experimental procedures used when conditioning animals.

The historical framework of classical conditioning

It was the physiologist Ivan Pavlov, while studying the salivary reflexes in dogs, who is recorded as being one of the first researchers to notice that an animal had formed an association between a previously **neutral stimulus** and a previously **unconditional** (unlearned) **response**. Thus, in the Fido example, the hated record would initially be the neutral stimulus, as before it has been paired with the neighbour's cat it does not cause the dog to whine.

As part of his research on salivation (production of saliva) in dogs Pavlov invented an apparatus to enable him to measure precisely the amount of saliva a dog produces. And in order to make the dog salivate so he could measure the saliva he gave it food – which, as we have seen, is an innate response to the sight of food when an animal is hungry. As no learning is involved in the reflexive salivation response Pavlov referred to this as an unconditional response (abbreviated to UCR) and referred to the food as an **unconditional stimulus** (abbreviated to UCS). Thus an unconditional stimulus and response are not conditional (dependent) on the learning of an association between two events.

In the course of studying dogs' salivation rates Pavlov (1927) noticed that after the research assistant (initially a neutral stimulus) had given the dogs food (initially a UCS) on a number of occasions the dogs began to salivate (initially a UCR) simply at the sight of the research assistant. Pavlov concluded that the dogs appeared to have formed an association between receiving food and the research assistant, thus salivating (**conditional response – CR**) at the sight of the assistant (now a **conditional stimulus – CS**). Hence the dog had formed an association between the food (UCS) and the research assistant (now an association has been formed, the CS) and therefore salivated simply at the sight of the research assistant. Consequently the research assistant was now a conditional stimulus and the salivation a conditional response because the salivation response was dependent (conditional) upon the research assistant being present.

Based on his observation of association learning Pavlov carried out a number of experiments to see if his conclusion was correct. So for the next specified number of 'feedings' Pavlov sounded a tone for a few seconds prior to giving the dogs their food and then measured the dogs' saliva production when this pairing (tone and food) occurred. After a number of pairings Pavlov sounded the tone but did not pair it with the food and again measured the dogs' saliva production. Pavlov found that the dogs still salivated at about the same rate as they did when the food was presented, thus supporting his original observation.

Pavlov then went on to carry out many controlled laboratory experiments to establish the general principles involved in classical conditioning, as well as developing the terminology involved in the explanation. These will now be considered.

The basic principles of classical conditioning

The acquisition (learning) of a response in classical conditioning

Pavlov went on to use a huge variety of stimuli to establish whether the animal would learn to associate them with food and therefore salivate when just the conditional stimuli were present. The typical experimental procedure is best understood by presenting verbal explanations accompanied by diagrams – hence both are used in the following experimental procedures used in classical conditioning. In doing this we will use a bell as the to-be-conditioned stimulus.

Stage 1: The animal is first presented with the to-be-conditioned stimulus (in this case a bell being rung), called the neutral stimulus (NS). This is a control procedure, used in order to ensure that this neutral stimulus does not cause the unconditional response (in this case salivation) to occur when it is presented alone. Of course, the animal will show some reflex response to the to-be-conditioned stimulus – for example, it may show an orienting response (e.g. turn its head towards the source of the sound) but should not show the unconditional reflex response (salivation). Thus the researcher presents the animal with a NS (in this case a bell) to establish that it does not produce the UCR (in this case salivation) (see Figure 3.1).

NS

The animal does not exhibit the salivation response when the bell is rung therefore the bell is seen as a neutral stimulus

Figure 3.1 **Stage 1: presentation of a stimulus to establish whether it is a neutral stimulus**

Stage 2: The animal is then presented with the unconditional stimulus (UCS), in this case meat, and exhibits an unconditional response, in this case the salivation reflex. The researcher therefore presents the animal with the UCS, in this case food, to establish whether it produces the UCR, in this case salivation (see Figure 3.2).

UCS UCR

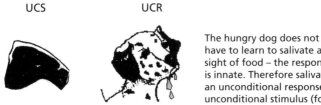

The hungry dog does not have to learn to salivate at the sight of food – the response is innate. Therefore salivation is an unconditional response to an unconditional stimulus (food)

Figure 3.2 **Stage 2: presentation of the unconditional stimulus**

Stage 3: The animal is now presented with the NS (in this case a bell) and the UCS (in this instance meat) in **temporal contiguity** (i.e. at the same time in the same place) on a number of consecutive occasions. Each time the animal is presented with these pairings (NS and UCS) it automatically produces the UCR (in this case the salivation reflex). Consequently the researcher presents the animal with NS (food), paired with UCS (bell), on a number of occasions (see Figure 3.3).

UCS NS

Figure 3.3 **Stage 3: pairing of the unconditional stimulus with the neutral stimulus**

Stage 4: After a number of pairings of the NS (bell) and the UCS (food) the animal is now presented with the NS alone, to which the animal generally produces the UCR (salivation response). Thus the researcher presents the animal with the bell (previously the NS) on its own and measures any salivation response (previously the UCR) (see Figure 3.4).

If the animal now exhibits the salivation response when only the bell is presented it has been conditioned to associate what was formally the NS with the receipt of food (reinforcer). Hence the bell (previously the NS) has become a conditional (learned) stimulus (CS), and the

Conditional
Stimulus (CS)

Conditional
Response (CR)

The animal is now
salivating (CR) at the
presentation of the bell
alone (CS)

Figure 3.4 **Stage 4: presentation of the originally neutral stimulus
without the unconditional stimulus**

salivation response (previously a UCR) to this is now called the
conditional (learned) response (CR) – that is, the salivation response
is now conditional upon the animal hearing the bell being rung.

Progress exercise

Using the following example and the 'choice box' complete the following:
When I first got my dog I took her to the vet for her first injections. The vet
was very clumsy and hurt her, causing her to cower and yelp in pain. When
I took her back for two other injections he was again clumsy and hurt her.
Now, when we just pass by the vet's surgery, she cowers and yelps and tries
to get away from it.

		Choice box:
The NS was the	....	Injection
The UCS was the	....	Vet
The UCR was the	....	Vet's surgery
The CS was the	....	Pain
The CR was the	....	Cowering and yelping

Now check the answers to these at the back of this book to see if you were
correct.

Pavlov did many experiments using this procedure and discovered
many more things about the learning process via classical conditioning.
These are as follows:

Stimulus generalisation

Pavlov wondered how an animal would respond to stimuli that were fairly similar to the CS and carried out a number of experiments to establish what they were. He found that animals would produce the CR to any stimuli that were similar to the CS. For example, if the CS was the sound of a particular bell then the animal would exhibit the CR whenever it heard any similar bell. Pavlov discovered that the more similar the other stimuli were to the original CS, the stronger the CR the animal emitted; the less similar the stimuli were to the original CS, the weaker the CR. This is called a 'generalisation gradient'. For example, if the original CS was a bell of 5 decibels and the CR was salivation, then a bell of 4 or 6 decibels would cause much greater salivation than a bell of 1 or 9 decibels. However, Pavlov also discovered that animals were able to learn to discriminate (i.e. tell the difference) between stimuli.

Stimulus discrimination

Pavlov discovered that animals could learn to differentiate between similar stimuli – that is, they could learn stimulus discrimination. He showed that stimulus discrimination was learned in very much the same way as the acquisition of an association between things. How animals learn to discriminate was shown using the following experimental procedure:

Stage 1 (control stage): First, the animal is first presented with the to-be-conditioned NS (for example a bell of 5 decibels), to which the animal shows an orienting response.

Stage 2: The animal is then presented with the UCS (meat); the animal exhibits the UCR (salivation reflex) when presented with the meat.

Stage 3: The animal is now presented with the bell of 5 decibels and the UCS (meat) in temporal contiguity (i.e. at the same time in the same place) on a number of consecutive occasions. Each time the animal is presented with these pairings (NS and UCS) it exhibits the UCR (salivating reflex).

Stage 4: The animal is now presented with the bell of 5 decibels alone, and salivates. It has thus been conditioned to produce the salivation response (CR) to the sound of the bell of 5 decibels (CS).

Note that it is at this stage that the animal will show stimulus generalisation and may produce salivation to the sound of almost any bell. This is much like the teacher who 'monitors' at the sound of the school bell and the doorbell – he has generalised from the original school bell to his own doorbell. If he is to stop monitoring his family when the doorbell rings he must learn stimulus discrimination!

Stage 5: The animal is now presented with bells of various decibels on a number of occasions but only receives food when the bell of 5 decibels is presented.

Stage 6: The animal is now presented with the bells of different decibels, and it is found that it only exhibits the CR (salivation reflex) with the bell of 5 decibels. Thus it shows stimulus discrimination: it is able to detect the difference between the sound of the bell that will lead to reinforcement (food) and those that will not, and therefore only responds to the stimulus that will result in reinforcement.

Higher-order or second-order conditioning

Pavlov also discovered that things other than the UCS could become associated; specifically, he found that a CS could be used to condition a *second* UCS. For example, after conditioning an animal to produce a certain CR (e.g. salivation) to a CS (e.g. a bell – the original (first-order) CS). This is known as **higher-order or second-order conditioning**.

He discovered that, like stimulus generalisation and discrimination, the processes involved in second- or higher-order conditioning act in very similar ways to the acquisition process. The experimental procedures which show how second/higher-order conditioning occurs are as follows:

Stage 1: This is the acquisitions stage. It proceeds exactly as in the basic example of classical conditioning procedure (stages 1 through to 4). Hence, in this example, the animal is conditioned to salivate when a bell is rung; thus the bell is now the CS and salivation is now the CR.

Stage 2: This CS (bell) is now paired, in close temporal contiguity, and on a number of occasions, with a second UCS – for example, a triangle, but without the original UCS (food) being presented at the same time (see Figure 3.5). Thus it proceeds to Stage 3.

Stage 3: The second-order UCS is now presented on its own to see if it causes the CR. Thus in this case the researcher presents the animal

CS   Second-order UCS

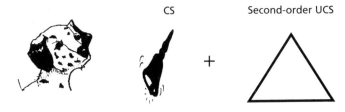

Figure 3.5 **Stage 1: pairing of the conditional stimulus with a second unconditional stimulus**

with the triangle to establish whether it produces the CR (that is, whether it salivates).

Second-order CS   Second-order CR

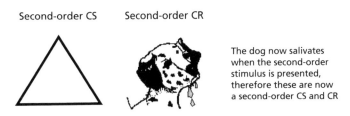

The dog now salivates when the second-order stimulus is presented, therefore these are now a second-order CS and CR

Figure 3.6 **Stage 2: presentation of the second-order conditional stimulus**

Extinction

Pavlov also discovered how behaviour previously learned through classical conditioning can also be unlearned or, to use the appropriate terminology, can be extinguished. To be more precise, extinction is when an animal learns *not* to respond to a stimulus any more.

Extinction happens if we present the CS on a number of occasions in the absence of the UCS – that is, for example, we present Pavlov's dog with a ringing bell on a number of occasions but do not present any food (i.e. do not pair the CS with the UCS). It seems that the animal now learns a new association in that it appears to understand that the ringing bell is no longer associated with the receipt of food; consequently the salivation production begins to lessen on each presentation of the CS without the UCS until it simply disappears. Hence extinction is not a sudden process, but occurs slowly in that the CR slowly becomes progressively weaker until it no longer occurs.

However, extinction is not as straightforward as this account would have us believe – Pavlov found that carrying out an extinction procedure did not lead to total loss of the learned association.

Spontaneous recovery

Pavlov found that when a response appears to have been extinguished, in that it is no longer exhibited when the animal is presented with the CS, if the CS is presented again some time later the animal might show the CR again – albeit in a much weaker form. This is known as **spontaneous recovery**.

Pavlov found that to extinguish a CR fully the CS should be presented on a number of occasions. If this is done the CR gets weaker and weaker each time the CS is presented until it no longer elicits the CR whenever the CS is presented. Nevertheless, even when the CR has been completely extinguished research has shown that, compared to naive animals (i.e. animals which have never been conditioned to exhibit a particular response), previously conditioned animals who have had the CR completely extinguished will re-learn the response much faster than naive animals learn it. Therefore it would seem that the learning is never entirely forgotten.

Factors that influence the strength of a CR

Pavlov's research also revealed the factors that influence the strength of a CR. These are:

- The intensity of the UCS.
- The order and timing of the NS and UCS.

THE INTENSITY OF THE UCS

Pavlov found that the stronger the UCS the stronger the CR, and vice versa. This can be made clearer by using the previous dog salivation example: if the bell were rung quietly this would not produce nearly as much salivation as if the bell were rung loudly.

The order and timing of the NS and UCS are important – that is, the *temporal contiguity of presentation of the US and UCS*. Pavlov found that the most effective order and time gap between the presentation of the CS and UCS were, respectively, when the NS was presented half a second before the UCS and remained until the UCR appeared; this resulted in the most effective learning procedure. This format of presentation of the NS and UCS is known as **forward conditioning**. To make forward conditioning clearer an example would be when a bell is rung (NS) half a second before presenting an animal with food (UCS) and continues to be rung until the animal salivates. This form of presentation would result in the greatest amount of salivation (CR) when, after a number of pairings, the bell is presented alone. Pavlov found that learning becomes poorer if the time gap between the presentation of the NS and UCS increases beyond the optimal half a second; this format of presentation is referred to as **delayed conditioning**. Pavlov also found that **backward conditioning**, whereby the NS is presented just before the UCS, occurs.

Evaluation of classical conditioning

An adequate theory of classical conditioning must explain why Pavlov's dogs began salivating to the CS; indeed, Pavlov's own explanation can clearly do this. The explanation claims that salivation is part of a set of involuntary responses elicited by food, and as a consequence of the researcher pairing a CS with the delivery of food the animal comes to associate the two events. This association of these two events ensures that the presentation of one of them will activate the presentation of the other. Therefore this activation will elicit salivation just as it would have if it had been elicited by the presentation of food itself. Evidence clearly supports this explanation.

Classical conditioning is clearly able to explain how some simple forms of learning might occur. Nevertheless, it is very limited because it is only able to explain associations with involuntary behaviours (i.e. ones that the animal has no real control over, such as fear) that an animal already has. However, a great deal of learning is both novel and much more complex than this, involving voluntary as well as involuntary responses, and therefore cannot be explained by classical conditioning.

Classical conditioning cannot explain one-trial learning that only involves one pairing of a UCS and CS for an association to be formed – for example, taste aversion studies where an emetic (something that makes the animal sick) is paired with a specific food just once to cause the animal to avoid that food in future (Garcia and Koelling, 1966). Consider: this theory claims that a number of pairings of an NS and UCS are necessary in order to learn that the NS can elicit the CR. Yet in one-trial learning just one pairing of an NS with a UCS is all that is needed for an animal to make an association.

Classical conditioning theory's assumption that an association can be formed between *any* NS and UCS, as long as they are paired together on a number of occasions using forward conditioning with a half-second time gap between the presentation of the NS and the UCS, also appears to be incorrect. Research has clearly shown that some associations are learned much more readily than others; specifically, research has shown that animals appear to be biologically prepared to learn some associations very quickly (Grier and Burk, 1992) – the association in the taste aversion study, for example.

The historical framework of operant conditioning

As with classical conditioning, the theoretical assumptions of operant conditioning also developed from a historical framework. Just after the turn of the century, at about the same time that Pavlov was conducting his experiments on classical conditioning, Edward L. Thorndike (1911), an American psychologist, was carrying out his own research into learning in animals.

Thorndike stated that an animal's responses are modified by the consequences of the behaviour whereby a positive consequence (desirable outcome) increases the probability that a given behaviour will be performed again and a negative consequence (undesirable outcome) decreases the probability that a given behaviour will be performed again. Thus the action performed by an animal is dependent on the outcome of performing it.

Thorndike further stated that 'When particular stimulus–response sequences are followed by pleasure, those responses tend to be "stamped in"; responses followed by pain tend to be "stamped out".' The final interpretation of the law of effect was that the immediate consequence of a mental connection could work back upon it to strengthen it. Consequently, it was Thorndike's law of effect that formed the basis for his theory of instrumental conditioning, the forerunner of operant conditioning (see p. 62).

Thorndike's theory of instrumental conditioning

Thorndike formulated his theory from his observations of cats' trial-and-error learning to enable them to escape from puzzle boxes to obtain food. In such studies of trial-and-error learning Thorndike would typically place a hungry cat in a puzzle box (which he invented for these studies). Once in the puzzle box the cat would be able to see a dish of food outside the puzzle box – this was its incentive to escape. Inside the puzzle box Thorndike had rigged up a number of devices that, if pulled or pushed, would lead to the puzzle box door being opened, thus allowing the cat to escape and obtain the food (see Figure 3.7).

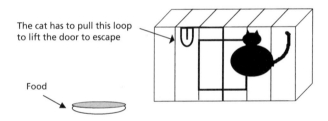

Figure 3.7 **Thorndike's puzzle box**

Thorndike observed that when a cat is first put into the puzzle box it initially tries squeezing through the bars. When it can't get through the bars it starts lashing out wildly and, by pure accident, it pulls the loop. As a consequence of this the cat gains freedom and food, thus positively reinforcing the loop-pulling behaviour. The cat is then returned to the puzzle box each time it escapes. Thorndike observed that after a number of trials (being placed in the puzzle box) the cat eventually learns to connect the pulling of the loop with escape and receipt of food. Thus, when the cat is placed back in the box, after a number of trials it goes straight to the loop, pulls it, and escapes. Therefore, according to Thorndike, the cat has now developed a connection between pulling the loop and positive consequences.

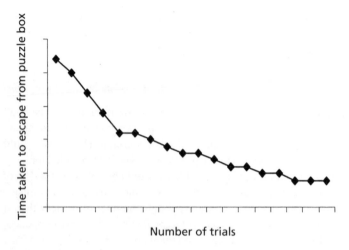

Figure 3.8 **Typical learning curve of a cat placed in Thorndike's puzzle box**

Thorndike studied several cats, and plotted the time it took for them to escape from the puzzle box on successive trials. He found that these learning curves (see Figure 3.9) did not suddenly improve; instead, the amount of time the animal spent in the box before it pulled the loop and escaped gradually shortened.

From these observations Thorndike claimed that the animal not only realised what it had to do to escape but also made a connection between its situation and the response that led to freedom. This eventually became 'stamped in' the animal's brain in the form of nerve connections. Based on these observations Thorndike proposed that certain stimuli and responses become connected or dissociated from each other according to his law of effect (see p. 61).

These observations led Thorndike to conclude that animals learn solely by trial and error (or success), or reward and punishment. Thorndike used the cat's behaviour in a puzzle box to describe what happens when all beings learn anything. According to Thorndike all learning involves the formation of connections and these connections are strengthened according to the law of effect. Thorndike's view of intelligence is that it is simply the ability to form connections, and as humans are the most evolved animals they form more connections than any other.

Thorndike's findings led him to formulate the principles of instrumental conditioning theory. This theory represents the original S–R framework of behaviourism in that it states that learning involves forming connections between stimuli and responses. According to Thorndike these connections are neuronal connections (connections made between nerves) within the brain. Consequently, he stated that learning is simply the process of the 'stamping in' or 'stamping out' of these stimulus–response connections – known as connectionism. The hallmark of connectionism (like all behaviourist theories) was that learning could be adequately explained without referring to any unobservable internal states such as thinking and perception. Therefore instrumental conditioning theory is very similar to classical conditioning theory in that they both hold that only observable behaviour should be studied to gain an understanding about how animals learn. However, the key difference between classical conditioning and instrumental conditioning is that classical conditioning states that learning involves associations between unconditioned reflex behaviours. Instrumental and operant conditioning (covered next), on the other hand, state that learning involves associations between the performance of specific behaviour and the consequences of these actions.

Thorndike's instrumental conditioning theory states that the following three main conditions are necessary for learning to occur: the **law of effect**, the **law of recency**, and the **law of exercise**.

The law of effect: This states that the strength of a connection between a stimulus and a response is influenced by the consequences of a response. Thorndike believed that successful consequences (i.e. pleasant ones) strengthened a connection. (A consequence of the law of effect is that responses that reduce the likelihood of achieving positive consequences (e.g. punishment, failures) would also decrease in strength.)

The law of recency: This states that the most recent response is likely to govern the recurrence of the response.

The law of exercise: This states that the strength of a connection is determined by how often the connection is used. It contains two portions: *law of use* (the strength of a connection increases when the connection is used); *law of disuse* (the strength of a connection diminishes when the connection is not used). Thus connections become strengthened with practice (repetition) and weakened when practice is discontinued.

The S–R associations and the corresponding laws of learning can be seen to occur in Thorndike's cat studies: after much trial and error behaviour the cat learns to associate pulling the loop (S) with escape from the box (R). This S–R connection is established because it results in a positive consequence (escape from the box and receipt of food). The law of exercise specifies that the connection was established because the S–R pairing occurred on many occasions (the law of exercise) and resulted in a positive consequence (law of effect), as well as forming a single sequence (law of readiness).

Evaluation of Thorndike's theory of instrumental conditioning

A number of flaws were found in Thorndike's theory and these led to a number of modifications in a bid to overcome them; consequently, Thorndike's theory is now only of historical importance. Skinner's modification of Thorndike's instrumental conditioning theory led to the formulation of a much better theory – operant conditioning theory.

Skinner's modification of Thorndike's theory of instrumental conditioning

Thorndike's instrumental conditioning theory was further developed and modified by B. F. Skinner in the 1930s (Skinner, 1938), the outcome being Skinner's formulation of **operant conditioning** theory.

Skinner felt that the study of learning should be more controlled and scientific, therefore he invented an apparatus known as the operant chamber or Skinner box, with a cumulative recording device incorporated (see Figure 3.9). This device enabled much more precise manipulation of stimuli, better control of the situation, and behaviour to be measured more easily and accurately. Using this device Skinner attempted to isolate and identify the basic components involved in instrumental conditioning so that the principles of learning could be unambiguously identified.

Skinner also changed the name of instrumental conditioning to 'operant conditioning' because he called the response which is rewarded the **operant**. An operant is any behaviour that is emitted by an animal that results in a change in the animal's environment – for example, lever-pressing that results in the receipt of food is an operant. This is because Skinner claimed that this type of learning was not the

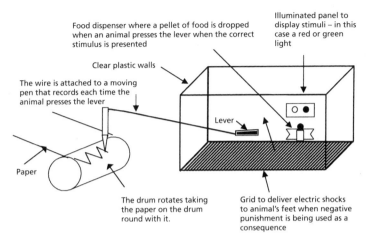

Food dispenser where a pellet of food is dropped when an animal presses the lever when the correct stimulus is presented

Illuminated panel to display stimuli – in this case a red or green light

Clear plastic walls

The wire is attached to a moving pen that records each time the animal presses the lever

Lever

Paper

The drum rotates taking the paper on the drum round with it.

Grid to deliver electric shocks to animal's feet when negative punishment is being used as a consequence

Figure 3.9 **Skinner box (operant chamber) and cumulative recording device**

result of a stimulus–response association but instead was an *association* between the operant response and the reinforcer (see below). This proposal is in contrast to Thorndike's earlier proposal that animals adapt to their environment by forming associations between stimuli (S) and responses (R).

Skinner was also responsible for renaming a positive consequence a 'reinforcer' and a negative consequence 'punishment'. Skinner also introduced a number of different types of reinforcers and the effect these may have on the likelihood that an animal will or will not perform a given behaviour again in similar circumstances. Skinner reasoned that there are two types of consequence, pleasant and unpleasant, each producing two consequences of performing a given behaviour (see Table 3.1).

Skinner also referred to two other types of reinforcer: (1) **primary reinforcer**; (2) **conditioned (or secondary) reinforcer**.

A primary reinforcer is one that is biologically pre-established to act as reinforcement. For example, food, water and sex are all primary reinforcers as they satisfy an animal's biological desires. Thus if a hungry bird pecks at the ground and this results in the receipt of worms this reward acts as a primary reinforcer and increases the probability that the bird will peck at the ground on other occasions when it is hungry.

Table 3.1 Skinner's types of reinforcement and their consequences

Type of consequence and Skinner's terminology	Skinner's terminology for consequence	General description of consequence and an example of it
Pleasant consequences known as reinforcement	Positive reinforcement	Something good can start or be presented; animal receives food
	Negative reinforcement	Something bad can end or be taken away; receipt of an electric shock stops
Unpleasant consequences known as punishment	Positive punishment	Something bad can start or be presented; receives an electric shock
	Negative punishment	Something good can end or be taken away; food is taken away

A conditioned (or secondary) reinforcer is a previously neutral stimulus (anything that stimulates the senses) that, if paired with a primary reinforcer, acquires the same reinforcement properties that are associated with the primary reinforcer. For example, the clicker is a device that, as the name suggests, makes a clicking noise and is used to train dogs. The clicker is often seen being used in TV programmes about pet behaviour problem-solving. The dog is positively reinforced using a primary reinforcer – food. Each time the dog exhibits the desired behaviour, for example sitting, it receives a tit-bit of food. When the dog has learned to perform the given behaviour a clicker is now sounded each time the dog sits, and at the same time the dog is positively reinforced by receiving the primary reinforcer – the tit-bit of food. Eventually the sound of the clicker becomes equivalent to the receipt of the primary reinforcer, therefore the sound of the clicker now acts as a reinforcer for sitting behaviour.

Skinner claims that these consequences effect the likelihood that an animal will or will not perform a given behaviour again in similar circumstances. The effects of each of these consequences are shown in Table 3.2, and it is important that they, and the terms used in this section, are understood.

Skinner also held that operant conditioning could not take place without a reinforcer.

Table 3.2 The role of reinforcers in operant conditioning		
Type of consequence	Effect on performance of given behaviour	
Reinforcement	Positive reinforcement *increases* the probability that the behaviour will be performed again under similar circumstances. Therefore it *strengthens* behaviour.	Positive punishment *decreases* the probability that the behaviour will be performed again under similar circumstances. Therefore it *weakens* behaviour.
Punishment	Negative reinforcement *increases* the probability that the behaviour will be performed again under similar circumstances. Therefore it *strengthens* behaviour.	Negative punishment *decreases* the probability that the behaviour will be performed again under similar circumstances. Therefore it *weakens* behaviour.

The nature of operant conditioning and its role in the behaviour of animals

In sum, according to operant conditioning theory, learning is due to the link formed between an action and the consequence(s) of performing the action. Moreover, if an action produces pleasant consequences it is much more likely to be performed again, but if the consequences are undesirable it is less likely to be performed again. Consequently, operant conditioning is based on the **law of reinforcement** which states that the probability of a given response being emitted is increased if the consequences of performing it are pleasant.

The law of reinforcement applies to all cases of learning, and operant conditioning is therefore different from classical conditioning. Unlike in classical conditioning, where a new response is created by associating it with a UCS, in operant conditioning there is no creation of a new response to a neutral stimulus. Instead, in operant conditioning there is an increase or decrease in a response that is already being exhibited.

The procedures involved in operant conditioning research

In the Skinner box a rat may have to learn to press the lever to either gain food (positive reinforcement), end an electric shock (**negative reinforcement**), stop food being taken away (**negative punishment**) or prevent the receipt of an electric shock (**positive punishment**).

The acquisition of a response in operant conditioning

When the rat is placed in the Skinner box initially (understandably) the animal appears to be wary of the new situation and begins to 'explore' the Skinner box, wandering around and sniffing at things. During this 'exploration' the rat may accidentally press the lever (operant). This accidental occurrence enables the researcher to manipulate the consequences of the rat's accidental lever-pressing behaviour by making the consequences of this either pleasant or unpleasant.

Skinner showed that if the researcher positively reinforces or negatively reinforces the rat's accidental lever-pressing behaviour (i.e. positive consequences) then it resulted in an *increase* in lever pressing by the rat. However if the researcher used positive or negative punishment (an unpleasant consequence) the lever pressing behaviour quickly *decreases* and then stops. Therefore these findings clearly support the law of effect.

Note from the above procedure that unlike Thorndike, who used 'trials' in instrumental conditioning, Skinner's operant conditioning procedure does not use trials – instead, the researcher has waited for the animal to emit a particular response, which is then either reinforced or punished. However, waiting until trial and error results in an animal performing the desired response so that this response could be reinforced or punished to show operant conditioning could be exceedingly time consuming – especially with complex behaviours such as only pressing the lever when a green light comes on. Therefore Skinner devised a behaviour-shaping procedure.

The acquisition of a response in operant conditioning using behaviour shaping

In the shaping procedure the animal (usually a rat or a pigeon) is placed in a Skinner box. If the desired acquisition response were, for example, pressing a lever in the Skinner box then the researcher would 'shape' this behaviour as follows. Initially the animal is positively reinforced (e.g. given food) for producing any behaviour that approximates (resembles) the desired lever-pressing behaviour. For example, in a simplified procedure the animal will initially 'explore' the operant chamber, moving about, sniffing, leaning against walls, etc. So, for example, whenever the animal faces the wall with the lever on it can be given a positive reinforcer (e.g. food), hence increasing the probability that the animal will face that wall as opposed to the other three. This **positive reinforcement** will now be given on a number of occasions until the animal spends most of its time facing the wall with the lever on it. When this desired behaviour has been acquired positive reinforcement of this behaviour is then stopped. Now another behaviour that is nearer the desired behaviour is positively reinforced – for example, approaching the lever on the wall. Again when the animal begins to spend most of its time around the lever this behaviour will stop being positively reinforced. Now another behaviour that is nearer still to the desired behaviour is now positively reinforced, such as sniffing the lever, then touching the lever, until eventually only the pressing of the lever by the animal will be positively reinforced. Hence the animal's behaviour has been 'shaped' so that reinforcement causes it to perform successively nearer approximations of the desired behaviour until eventually it only performs the desired behaviour – in this case lever pressing. This finding also supports the law of effect.

Skinner's shaping procedures clearly show how reinforcement results in learning a specific response. The process of behaviour shaping is very important for two reasons:

1 It has shown how novel behaviours in animals may be learned. Classical conditioning is unlike this in that it is only able to explain behaviours that an animal already has.
2 It can show how voluntary and involuntary behaviours influence learning, while classical conditioning can only explain association learning of involuntary behaviour.

The behaviour-shaping procedure has also been used to study a number of operant conditioning phenomena, which will now be considered.

Generalisation

Just as in classical conditioning it would appear that generalisation is also a feature of operant conditioning. In operant conditioning the animal often exhibits a variety of responses that are similar to the acquired response or responses that the animal has been shaped to exhibit. For example, if the required response is pressing the lever with its right front paw then the animal may show a number of responses that are similar to the required response – pressing the lever with its left front paw, with both paws, with its nose, or only half pressing the lever instead of fully pressing it until it clicks; this is called **response generalisation**. However, if these response generalisations are not reinforced and/or are punished then the animal will learn to discriminate (see below) and eventually exhibit the behaviours that are reinforced.

The animal will also exhibit a very similar response(s) to stimuli that are similar but not identical to the original stimulus – this is called **stimulus generalisation**. For example, if a rat is reinforced whenever it presses a red lever it will also attempt to press a number of different coloured levers in a Skinner box. Furthermore, the more similar the stimulus is to the original the greater the frequency of responses the animal will emit. Thus if the original lever was deep red then the animal will also press levers of varying shades of red. However, it will press a lever that is nearest to the original shade of red (e.g. crimson) more times, per minute, than a lever that is least like the original shade of red (e.g. pink). As with response generalisations, if these stimulus generalisation behaviours are not reinforced and/or are punished the animal learns to discriminate, eventually only pressing the original stimulus lever.

Discrimination

Like generalisation, **stimulus discrimination** learning also appears to occur in both classical and operant conditioning in a very similar way. Thus, if only a very specific response is reinforced eventually the animal will only exhibit this specific response. For example, if a rat is only reinforced when it presses the lever until it clicks with its front right paw, or only when it presses a dark-red lever, then after a few trials the rat will only exhibit this specific behaviour. Consequently, it will result in the elimination of any response generalisations (such as half pressing the lever or pressing it with its left front paw) and any stimulus generalisation (such as pressing a variety of levers of a different shade of red).

Extinction

As we have seen in classical conditioning, if a UCS is no longer presented with the CS, eventually the CR will decrease until it disappears – or extinguishes. It appears that a very similar process occurs in operant conditioning in that if a reinforcer no longer follows behaviour then the learned behaviour weakens and eventually extinguishes.

Spontaneous recovery

This also appears to operate in operant conditioning in the same way that it operates in classical conditioning. For example, if an animal has learned to press a lever only when a red light comes on to receive food this behaviour can be extinguished as follows. Whenever the animal presses the lever when the red light comes on the animal is no longer reinforced with the receipt of food. Thus, failing to reinforce the lever-pressing behaviour with food when the red light is on reduces the performance of this behaviour until eventually the animal does not show this behaviour. However, if the animal is placed in the same situation some time after this behaviour has stopped and the red light is illuminated then the animal begins pressing the lever again.

Factors that influence a conditional response

It has already been seen that Skinner's research has clearly shown that reinforcers influence behaviour and that a response cannot be conditioned without a reinforcer – hence the response/behaviour is conditional upon the reinforcer. However, Skinner also manipulated the timing and schedules of reinforcement to establish the effects of this on learning. The findings gained from these manipulations are one of Skinner's most important contributions to our understanding of learning.

Factors that influence the strength of a conditioned response (CR)

In classical conditioning, research has shown that a conditioned response is influenced by two factors: (1) temporal contiguity and (2) the strength of the UCS. However, Skinner showed that while operant conditioning is also affected in similar ways instead of temporal contiguity and the strength of the UCS it is the following two factors that influence the strength of a CR:

1 Ratio (proportion) of reinforcement.
2 The time interval (delay) between response and reinforcement.

Skinner further established that these two variables – ratio and interval – could be changed in two ways. That is, they could be:

1 fixed (i.e. the same every time), or
2 variable (i.e. changeable).

Skinner manipulated these variables to produce five types of schedules of reinforcement:

1 Continuous schedule.
2 Fixed-ratio schedule.
3 Variable-ratio schedule.

4 Fixed-interval schedule.
5 Variable-interval schedule.

Skinner's research showed that each specific type of schedule resulted in different effects on conditioning. The description and effects of each of these types of schedule, together with an example of each, can be seen in Table 3.3.

Consider how an animal in its natural environment may experience Skinner's schedules of reinforcement in everyday life.

Progress exercise

An evaluation of operant conditioning

An adequate account of operant conditioning must explain the conditions under which a response will be emitted on future occasions and when it will not be emitted. Skinner's account clearly does this. The explanation states that the probability of a behaviour being repeated or not being repeated can be predicted by the consequence(s) of performing a given behaviour, and evidence clearly supports this explanation.

Nevertheless, operant conditioning theory does have problems in that there appear to be many other types of learning that it is unable to explain, such as observational learning, insight learning and latent learning (covered on pp. 76–79).

Operant conditioning theory claims that for reinforcement to be effective on animals it must be administered almost immediately after the animal has emitted the desired response. However, research has shown that this is not necessarily the case. For example, Mackintosh (1984) showed that rats are able to learn which of two pathways in a maze leads to reinforcement in the form of food, even when there is a delay of several seconds between the maze pathway choice and the receipt of food.

Table 3.3 Types of schedules of reinforcement, together with a description, an example, and the effectiveness of each

Schedule	Features of schedule	Example	Effectiveness
1 Continuous	Reinforcement is given for every desired response almost immediately. It is usually used in the early part of a conditioning procedure.	An animal is given a food pellet every time it presses a lever.	This produces very effective conditioning but it extinguishes very quickly. This is probably because the animal has learned to predict that reinforcement will occur on every occasion; when reinforcement is not forthcoming it only takes a few non-reinforced trials to realise that the behaviour will no longer result in pleasant consequences.
2 Fixed ratio	Reinforcement is given after a fixed number of desired responses have been emitted. For example, after every five presses of a lever.	An animal is given a food pellet for every fifth press of the lever.	This produces a fast, steady rate of response but it extinguishes very quickly; thus, this schedule is not that effective. The ineffectiveness is probably because the animal is able to learn how many responses are required for reinforcement and when this no longer occurs it quickly learns that the response no longer produces a pleasurable consequence.
3 Variable ratio	Reinforcement is given after an average number of desired responses have been emitted – for example, if the average response ratio is ten then reinforcement will not be administered every tenth response, but the animal will receive ten reinforcements for every 100 responses.	An animal is given a food pellet after 7, 12, 8, then 13 presses of the lever, resulting in an average of ten responses for reinforcement to occur.	This produces a fast, steady rate of response and it is highly resistant to extinction; thus this schedule is very effective. Its effectiveness is probably because it is not possible for the animal to learn the precise number of responses required for reinforcement to occur, therefore it simply carries on emitting the lever-pressing response.

4	Fixed interval	This schedule reinforces the first appropriate response that occurs after a fixed period of time (e.g. after two minutes) and then every consecutive same time period (e.g. every two minutes). Thus, the animal has to learn to emit the appropriate response after a fixed period of time (e.g. every two minutes).	The animal is given a food pellet two minutes after it presses the lever throughout the trial.	This results in a slow rate of response – often only one response per interval – and the animal often only makes responses towards the last few seconds of the interval. Extinction is rapid; thus this schedule is not that effective. Its ineffectiveness is probably because the animal is able to learn the amount of time that will elapse before the response is reinforced and when this no longer occurs it quickly learns that the response no longer produces a pleasurable consequence.
5	Variable interval	Reinforcement is given after an average passage of time, provided that at least one desirable response has been emitted during this time period. For example, if the average time interval is five minutes then reinforcement will not be given at the end of every five-minute interval; however, ten reinforcements will be given in a fifty-minute period.	The animal is given a food pellet after six minutes, then four minutes, then three minutes, and then seven minutes after it has pressed the lever, resulting in an average time interval of five minutes between receipt of reinforcement.	This produces a fast, steady rate of response and is highly resistant to extinction; thus this schedule is highly effective. Its effectiveness is probably because it is not possible for the animal to learn the precise amount of time that will elapse before the response is reinforced, therefore it simply carries on emitting the lever-pressing response.

Finally, operant conditioning theory claims that learning cannot occur without reinforcement. Research has shown that this claim also appears to be incorrect. For example, Tolman and Honzik (1930) showed that rats could learn a route in a maze without obtaining reinforcement. They tested three groups of food-deprived rats in a maze apparatus. The rats in the first group were allowed to wander a maze once each day and obtained reinforcement in the form of food on reaching the end location. The rats in the second group were allowed to wander a maze once each day, but on reaching the end location received no reinforcement of food until the eleventh day. The rats in the third group acted as a control group and were allowed to wander a maze once each day, but on reaching the end location received no reinforcement of food. Findings showed that the rats in the first group quickly learnt the way through the maze, while the rats in the third group (no reinforcement) simply moved aimlessly around the maze. However, the rats in the second group moved about the maze somewhat aimlessly during the first eleven days, but when they received reinforcement they learned the maze even faster than the rats in the first group. Therefore it appears that the rats in the second group had in fact learned the correct route in the maze before reinforcement was given because they were able to select the appropriate route much faster than the rats in the first group, consequently showing that learning can occur in the absence of reinforcement. This type of learning is known as latent learning and is considered on pp. 78–79.

An evaluation of classical and operant conditioning

Without a doubt operant and classical conditioning theories are among the greatest successes in psychology. Researchers and theorists have identified many determinants of behaviour that enable us to describe and predict behaviour across species as well as across experimental settings. These established determinants are not only valued for their theoretical enlightenment but also for their application in understanding behaviour in everyday life situations. Nevertheless few, if any, theories go unchallenged in psychology and conditioning theories are no exception.

Conditioning theories dominated psychological thinking from the early part of last century to the mid-1960s, when many researchers started to become increasingly dissatisfied with them. This was mainly due to their claim that mental processes were simply epiphenomena (useless by-products) that played no role in determining an animal's behaviour. Unlike Pavlov, Skinner and other behaviourists, the anti-behaviourists claimed that internal mental processes, such as perception, thinking and emotion, in fact played a crucial role in determining an animal's behaviour; this can clearly be seen in insight learning and latent learning.

Another major criticism of conditioning as a determinant of animal behaviour is behaviourists' rigid claim that environmental factors are the major determinants of animal behaviour, plus their consequent denial that biological factors play any significant role. However, recent research (e.g. Gould and Marler, 1987) has shown that biological factors do play a significant role in classical and operant conditioning. Such research has shown that animals appear to be biologically prepared (i.e. a biologically determined readiness to learn some associations and not others) to learn some associations much more readily than others. Thus, even when one behaviour is reinforced many more times than another behaviour an animal will learn the less-reinforced behaviour much more quickly and efficiently than the most-reinforced behaviour. For example, Gould and Marler (1987) showed that bees could be readily conditioned to feed from a specific type of flower using the smell of the flower (discriminative stimulus) to distinguish it from other types of flower. However, they found that it was much harder to condition this behaviour using the colour of the flower (discriminative stimulus) to distinguish it from other types of flower. These researchers found that it is even more difficult to condition this behaviour using the shape of the flower (discriminative stimulus) to distinguish it from other types of flower, and almost impossible to condition this behaviour using other distinguishing criteria.

Indeed, Skinner found that it was far easier to train a rat to press a lever with its front paws to obtain food than it was to train it to press the lever with its back paws. While this is possible it requires much longer and more complex training. Furthermore, research has shown that rats will learn to avoid specific food on the basis of taste but not appearance. Such studies have shown that animals demonstrate an **associative bias** (i.e. a tendency to form some associations more readily than others), thus offering support for **biological preparedness**.

Research with animals and humans has shown that classical and operant learning occur in both the laboratory and the natural world.

However, research has also shown that most animal (and human) behaviour in the real world is much more complex than either classical or operant conditioning theory would suggest (as we shall see in the next chapter). Furthermore, learning in the real world involves much more than associations and reinforcement. Rather than concentrating on the formation of associations, the role of reinforcement and the importance of contiguity and predictability therefore, it may be more useful to establish how animals learn to distinguish chance events from cause–effect events, and how animals balance these two events in the real world.

Criticisms have also been aimed at the procedures used in research to show how classical and operant conditioning can determine new behaviours; the main criticisms are as follows. In relative terms, classical and operant theories of learning are typically based on some very simple experimental procedures. Thus it is not really plausible to suppose that the same simple processes that are sufficient to explain learning that occurs under experimental conditions are sufficient to explain all forms of learning in the natural environment. This is because animals are constantly being bombarded by a multitude of stimuli at any given time in the real world and potentially could make hundreds of associations and/or experience multiple reinforcements. Consequently such research lacks ecological validity.

A further criticism of the methodology is the fact that most of the research into classical and operant conditioning has been done on animals – mainly rats and pigeons in operant and a variety of animals in classical. Findings using animals are then extrapolated (inferred more widely from a limited range of known facts) to humans. And while similar findings have been found using humans, more recent research suggests that there are important qualitative and quantitative differences in the way different species learn; therefore this remains a hugely debated issue. While conditioning theories have given us a great deal of understanding about the learning process, in reality they do not appear to have given us a clear understanding of all of the processes involved in the learning – particularly in the real world.

Although conditioning theories can explain some simple learned behaviour in the natural environment they cannot explain all learning in the natural environment. Research has shown that there are a number of types of learning that neither classical nor operant conditioning theory can explain – for example, insight learning, latent learning, observational learning and imitation learning, all of which are covered later.

Finally, on a positive point, while classical and operant conditioning theory are not complete explanations of learning their principles of learning have been successfully applied to everyday life, as can be seen in Chapters 1 and 5.

Types of learning classical and operant conditioning theory are unable to explain

A number of types of learning have been shown to occur in the real world that neither classical nor operant conditioning can explain. Furthermore, behaviourism's claim that mental processes play no important role in determining behaviour also fails to be supported by the following types of learning.

INSIGHT LEARNING

Insight learning involves an animal appearing to produce some new behaviour without any previous trial-and-error learning or other **associative learning** but instead via some internal manipulation of the representation of its environment. For example, probably the most celebrated studies are Köhler's (1925) series of experiments with chimpanzees that appeared to show they use planning and foresight; that is, cognitive reasoning (mental processes) to solve a problem. Köhler devised an arrangement in which all of the elements necessary for the solution of the problem were in full view of the animal. In one case, Köhler first showed a chimpanzee called Sultan how to use a stick to obtain a banana placed out of reach outside his cage. Köhler then placed two short bamboo canes outside of Sultan's cage, together with a banana that was placed out of reach of Sultan even when using one bamboo cane as an extension of his arm. What Sultan had to work out was how a means could be devised so that it was able to reach the banana. Köhler then observed Sultan's response. He found that initially the chimpanzee tried to reach the banana by using his arm, followed by one of the two bamboo canes. On failing to reach the bananas with either his arm or a bamboo stick (i.e. by use of trial-and-error learning) Sultan then sat back and looked in turn at the banana then the bamboo canes as if he were thinking about the situation. Sultan did this for a number of days until one day he stood up, picked up both bamboo canes and inserted one into the hollow end of the other to make a much longer cane. He then used the extended cane to retrieve the banana.

Köhler stated that this type of learning was insight learning, claiming that Sultan had been able to solve the problem because he had formed a mental representation of the situation. Sultan then used his mental representation to make a number of mental manipulations to 'work out' the consequences of such manipulations. In doing so Sultan apparently understood that the mental manipulation of inserting one stick inside the other would render the sticks long enough for him to be able to reach the banana. Thus Köhler claimed that on realising this Sultan had suddenly jumped up and applied the mental manipulation. Neither classical nor operant conditioning can adequately explain how insight learning occurs. Nevertheless, while it is apparent that insight learning does indeed occur in animals research suggests that it is very limited and does not arise without an extensive period of experience, probably involving much trial-and-error learning.

LATENT LEARNING

Latent learning is when learning has occurred but there has been no observable change in an animal's behaviour. Consider for a moment that you have actually gained a great deal of knowledge that you may, as yet, not have been given the opportunity to use. For example, you may have travelled from home to school each school day and on your way, without necessarily trying, have learned many things: street names, car models, who lives where, the names of shops, pubs, etc., who you meet on the route, and many more things. However, you may not as yet have been in a situation that required you to show you had learned such knowledge – this is a form of latent learning. Latent learning poses a huge problem for conditioning explanations as it occurs in the absence of any reward and remains stored in memory until it is needed in the future.

Tolman's studies show that latent learning does indeed occur in animals. Actually the term 'latent learning' originated from a series of classic experiments carried out by Tolman *et al*. One example of these experiments showing latent learning has already been considered on p. 74 (Tolman and Honzik, 1930). Consequently, a simple stimulus–response association or reinforcement cannot explain such learning as it did not involve any reinforcement; therefore neither classical nor operant conditioning can explain such learning. Furthermore, if learning has occurred but the animal does not display this until it is reinforced then memory processes (mental processes) must play an important role in this type of learning. As a result, the role of cognition in determining animal behaviour in latent learning is very problematic for behaviourist conditioning explanations.

Equally as problematic for classical and operant conditioning theory is the finding that there is yet another type of learning besides insight and latent learning involving cognition that neither classical nor operant conditioning theory can explain – that is, observational learning.

As the name implies, observational learning is learning that occurs via the animal observing the consequences of another animal's behaviour rather than directly via an association between a stimulus and behaviour.

The reader is referred to Chapter 4, where the concept of observational learning and evidence for it, is considered in depth.

The biological importance of classical and operant conditioning

Both classical and operant conditioning are of great benefit to an animal in the real world as they increase the probability that it will perform appropriate behaviours in its environment, therefore increasing the probability that it will survive long enough to get its genes into the next generation. Thus they render an animal's behaviour more adaptive to its environment.

In terms of adaptive behaviour classical and operant conditioning have been found to have two biologically important purposes.

First, they provide an animal with the means to enable it to learn from past experience to recognise stimuli that can predict the occurrence of an event that will enable the animal to make an appropriate response quicker and probably more effectively than it would otherwise be able to. For example, the smell of a camper's fire may enable a fox to predict that there will be scraps of food left behind, or the sound of rain may enable a bird to predict that there will be plenty of worms coming to the soil's surface.

Second, and more important, both operant and classical conditioning enable previously neutral stimuli to acquire some of the properties of biologically important stimuli because they have become associated with each other. For example, rain (neutral stimulus) can become associated with obtaining worms (biologically important stimulus) because the two have become associated with each other, leading to a 'search for worms response' to be emitted by the animal. Consequently, this association will cause the animal's behaviour to be modified so that it is more adaptive than it may otherwise have been.

Similarities and differences in classical and operant conditioning

These can be summarised as follows:

Similarities

- Both are forms of conditioning that appear to involve the formation of associations. Classical conditioning involves the formation of an association between a stimulus and a response (S–R), whereas operant conditioning involves the formation between a response and a consequence.
- Both forms of conditioning involve contiguous associations of two events.
- Both involve stimulus generalisation, discrimination, extinction and spontaneous recovery.

Differences

- Classical conditioning can only be used to condition involuntary, reflexive behaviours whereas operant conditioning can be used to condition both voluntary and involuntary behaviours.
- In classical conditioning the response (e.g. salivation) is dependent on the presence of the UCS (e.g. food); in operant conditioning the reinforcement (e.g. food) depends upon the response (e.g. lever-pressing).
- In classical conditioning one type of reinforcement (UCS, e.g. food) is only able to elicit one response (e.g. salivation), whereas in operant conditioning one type of reinforcement (e.g. food) can be used to elicit a wide variety of responses, especially when using behaviour-shaping techniques.
- In classical conditioning little or no weakening of the reinforcement (UCS, e.g. food) can occur, otherwise the response is extinguished;

consequently schedules of reinforcement cannot be used to vary response and extinction rates. However, in operant conditioning weakening of the reinforcement can occur as the timing and frequency of the reinforcer can be varied by using schedules of reinforcement that result in variation of both the response and extinction rates.

Summary

We have clearly seen that classical and operant conditioning can adequately explain some learning in animals (and in humans); however, they are not a complete explanation because they fail to explain non-associative learning such as latent learning, insight and observational learning, including imitation. Thus the determinants of animal behaviour are far more complex than classical or operant conditioning theory would suggest. Consequently, a number of other explanations are necessary to gain a more complete understanding of the determinants of animal behaviour. Despite this, these theories have made an important contribution to our understanding of some of the determinants of animal behaviour – at least under certain conditions. However, in order to understand the determinants of animal behaviour in the real world fully we need to look at evolutionary and environmental factors. This is because more recent research has clearly indicated that, while environmental factors may well determine an animal's behaviour, these factors are often restricted by biological factors clearly seen in biological preparedness.

Further reading

Barker, L. M. (1997) *Learning and Behaviour* (2nd edn), Upper Saddle River, N.J.: Prentice-Hall. This text provides a thorough account of the psychology of learning and uses many interesting, well-referenced examples to illustrate the principles.

Domjan, M. (1993) *Domjan and Burkhard's The Principles of Learning and Behaviour* (3rd edn), Pacific Grove, Calif.: Brooks/Cole. This is a very readable text that does an excellent job of providing an in-depth description of the principles of learning that apply to both human and animals.

Tarpy, R. (1997) *Contemporary Learning Theory and Research*, Maidenhead: McGraw-Hill. This text provides a thorough account of the psychology of learning.

4

Social learning in animals

An introduction to social learning in animals

As we have seen in the chapters so far there are a number of determinants of animal behaviour – genetic inheritance, evolutionary processes and associative learning via the processes of classical and operant conditioning. Another determinant of behaviour is through social learning.

What is social learning?

Social learning refers to learning by observing others, making mental representations on what is seen and then using these to reproduce the observed behaviour at some point in the future if it is appropriate to do so.

Social learning occurs when other conspecifics (individuals of the same species) have a direct influence on the acquisition of a new behaviour or skill and can be by imitation, tutoring, mimicry and stimulus enhancement. It does not include contagion – that is, an animal copying a conspecific's already known behaviour because it does not involve a new behaviour or skill. An example of contagion is yawning, as many animals may copy it but because they already have this behaviour in their repertoire it is not classed as learning.

Imitation involves learning a new behaviour from a conspecific through observation alone, whereby the animal simply 'copies what it sees or hears'. For example, research by Herbert and Harsh (1944) has shown that an animal will escape from a puzzle box much quicker if it has observed a conspecific do this.

Tutoring is the acquisition of a new behaviour from a conspecific investing time and energy in passing the behaviour on. For example, Boesch (1991) observed chimpanzees showing offspring how to crack nuts with stones, which included the mother showing how to correctly position the 'hammer' and intact nuts and slowing down and modifying her nut cracking for the benefit of the youngsters.

Mimicry is similar to imitation, differing because it involves an animal copying another's behaviour but receiving no reward for doing so. For example, a wasp beetle (*Clytus arietis*), like a wasp, has black and yellow colouring; it also copies the way in which a wasp flies as predators avoid them because they mistake them for wasps that inflict pain when they sting (Wickler, 1968).

Stimulus enhancement involves one or more individuals, present in a learner's environment, bringing the learner's attention to environmental features that are of importance to conspecifics. That is, an animal is attracted to things that are attractive to conspecifics. Therefore learning may occur due to the animal's inquisitive nature. For example, McQuoid and Galef (1993) observed stimulus enhancement in jungle fowl, as these birds appear to have a natural curiosity for feeding bowls visited by conspecifics. Nevertheless, not all animals are prone to stimulus enhancement as research has shown that it can impair performance in some (e.g. Zentall, 1996).

While there are a number of ways in which social learning can occur it is not always easy to establish whether it has occurred through imitation, tutoring, mimicry or stimulus enhancement.

Social learning appears to involve some cognitive processes (e.g. memory). Furthermore, as we have seen with mimicry, neither reinforcement nor direct responses by an animal are necessary for this type of learning to occur. All that is required is that the potential learner pays close attention to another animal's behaviour and stores this information in their memory so that it can be retrieved for later use. Such learning would enable animals to acquire any number of new responses in a variety of situations where the behaviour of conspecifics can be observed. This type of learning can also occur even when the animals being observed are not even attempting to teach the observer anything in particular. Consequently, social learning means that animals can constantly learn by keeping their 'eyes and ears open'.

As many animal species live in groups, ranging from two or three animals to hundreds, such living arrangements create a potential for a social life. Social life is an enormous facilitator of an expanded repertoire of behaviour for two main reasons. First, because social life is full of opportunities to observe and imitate other conspecifics' behaviour; second, because it is full of interpersonal problems to be solved to ensure that individuals survive long enough to reproduce. For example, an animal may need to hide food from more dominant animals, 'keep track' of past interactions with other conspecifics, and plan ways of gaining limited resources (e.g. mates), etc. Consequently the challenges of social life go well beyond the usual environmental challenges to survive and reproduce and thus offer many more opportunities for social learning to occur.

Explanations relating to the role of social learning in animals

Social learning occurs in much the same way as conditioning, but instead of a direct experience of rewards and punishments the animal observes another animal's responses and records whether these result in reward or **punishment**. Therefore in social learning the consequences of a response are indirect as they are experienced by observing the outcome of another animal's behaviour, whereas in conditioning the consequences of a response are direct as they are gained through the animal's own experience. Consequently, if an animal observes another animal's response and it results in a reward then the observer is likely to imitate the behaviour; if it results in punishment, however, then the observer is less likely to imitate the behaviour.

What role does social learning play in determining animal behaviour?

Social learning is said to play a vital role in enhancing the survival of both the individual as well as the group because such learning enables the rapid reproduction of advantageous behaviours. If a conspecific is observed performing behaviours that enhance or are to the detriment of that individual's survival then others can learn those behaviours simply by observing the conspecific's responses and the consequences of these in given situations. Thus if a particular response results in a desirable consequence the animal can learn to imitate the behaviour, but if the consequence is undesirable they can learn not to imitate it. For example, if a rat observes another rat performing a certain act and as a result gains food then the observer rat can imitate the act and also gain food. However, if it observes another rat eating something (e.g. food baited with rat poison) and subsequently becoming ill or dying then the observer rat can learn to avoid such food – an option that would not be available to a non-social animal. As a result, the observer rat is increasing the probability that it will survive because of social learning.

It should be fairly obvious now that social learning is much faster and far less costly than trial-and-error learning. This is because trial-and-error learning takes much longer to acquire and often involves performing behaviours that may actually be detrimental to survival; indeed, they may even be terminal. Consider a trial-and-error approach to establishing which foods are safe to eat and which are not. This would be a very bad strategy to adopt as it could result in a significant reduction in the animal's fitness because this type of approach could lead to death. Furthermore, social learning can be culturally transmitted to the next and subsequent generations very rapidly and this cultural transmission of information would therefore enhance their survival.

Cultural and genetic inheritance

It could be said that cultural inheritance (i.e. learning from the group to which the animal belongs) is equivalent to genetic inheritance as, like genetic inheritance, it leads to a process of evolutionary change through survival of the fittest. Those animals that learn through observation can learn to imitate 'successful behaviour' and learn not to imitate 'unsuccessful behaviour'. This imitation of successful behaviour could therefore increase the probability that they will survive long enough to get their genes into the next generation. These 'successful' animals will subsequently pass this behaviour onto their offspring and other conspecifics in the social group. Those who fail to learn these survival-enhancing behaviours will be less likely to survive long enough to get their genes into the next generation. Consequently, the 'survival-enhancing behaviours' will become more and more prevalent, leading to evolutionary change.

Social learning and cultural transmission of such learning is therefore hugely beneficial to animals' survival, probably more so than genetic transmission of survival-enhancing characteristics – for two reasons. First, learning through social and cultural transmission (passed on from the members of the group to which an animal belongs) means information can be transmitted far more quickly than it can be through genetic transmission, which can only occur with each new generation only. Second, such rapid changes produced by social learning and cultural transmission can also lead to huge changes in a very wide range of behaviours, unlike genetic transmission which usually only involves small modifications in a smaller range of behaviours in each successive generation.

Write a definition of social learning. State four reasons why social learning may be beneficial to an animal's survival. When you have done these tasks check your answers against the text.

Progress exercise

Research studies on social learning in animals

In order to demonstrate that social learning is apparent in animals we need evidence of such behaviour. Therefore we will now look at naturalistic observational research evidence and experimental evidence.

Naturalistic observational research as evidence for social learning in animals

Social learning in snow monkeys

Probably one of the clearest instances of social learning (and cultural transmission) in the natural environment was observed by Kawai (1965). Kawai was carrying out a naturalistic observational study of social behaviour in a troop of Japanese snow monkeys (a type of macaque monkey) on a small Japanese island (Koshima Islet). In order to encourage the monkeys to come out of the forest and onto the open beach, where they could be observed more easily, the researcher left a regular supply of food that included sweet potatoes and wheat. The monkeys quickly learned that the beach was a good source of food and spent more and more time there.

Kawai observed this troop over many years and during this time saw a two-year-old female, named Imo, do something remarkable. In a flash of inspiration (i.e. insight learning), she took her sweet potato to the water's edge and washed off the mud and sand on it. On finding that the potato tasted much better (presumably) she washed all her sweet potatoes before eating them from then on. The key finding was that very shortly after Imo's innovative potato-washing behaviour other monkeys in the troop appeared to imitate this; in a relatively short period over 80 per cent of the troop aged between two and seven years were washing their sweet potatoes before they ate them. However, only 18 per cent of the monkeys over the age of eight years imitated Imo's potato-washing behaviour. This is an important factor as it is thought to be due to the fact that the younger monkeys in the troop interact with each other much more than do the older ones. Therefore the younger monkeys had more opportunity to observe this behaviour occurring than the older monkeys did – that is, it is an example of social learning. However, the learning of this skill could also be partly due to the fact that younger monkeys are more willing to explore new skills than older monkeys, or, as will be considered later, the learning of this skill may simply be a case of associative learning.

Imo's innovative behaviour did not end with potato washing. Some two years later, again probably in a moment of insight, she was observed grabbing a handful of wheat off the beach – in fact a mixture of sand and wheat – and throwing it into the sea. She waited as the sand sank and the wheat floated and then simply scooped the clean wheat off the top of the water and ate it. From this point onwards Imo ate her wheat in this manner. Prior to this the monkeys had picked up each grain of wheat individually, which is a time-consuming and laborious task and thus more costly in terms of energy used in relation to the energy gained.

This wheat-skimming behaviour is much more astonishing than potato washing because potato washing is not radically different from behaviour exhibited in all macaques – brushing the sand and mud off potatoes with their hands before eating them. However, the separation of wheat and sand is radically different from the 'normal' behaviour of macaques, as it requires food to be acquired and then thrown away, waiting for the sand to sink and then re-acquiring the food.

As with the potato washing, within a relatively short time over 80 per cent of other two- to seven-year-old monkeys and 18 per cent of the older monkeys in the troop imitated Imo's wheat-skimming behaviour. Furthermore, both of Imo's apparent innovative behaviours were very quickly integrated into the troop's culture and from then on were culturally transmitted to subsequent generations. Today all members of this troop wash their sweet potatoes before eating them and forage for wheat using Imo's wheat-skimming technique.

Social learning in tits

Another example of social learning (and cultural transmission) in animals can be seen in the habit of opening milk-bottle tops to gain food in birds. This habit is most prolific in British tits, in particular great tits (*Parus major*) and blue tits (*Parus caerulus*), but it is apparent in other species of bird.

Fisher and Hinde (1948) were the first researchers to collect systematic reports of milk-bottle-top opening in birds. This behaviour was first described near Southampton, England, in 1921 where birds were observed pecking at and removing the foil tops from milk bottles and drinking the milk. Fisher and Hinde noted that through the 1930s and 1940s this behaviour spread rapidly throughout Britain – far too quickly for natural selection to have been 'at work'. Consider that prior to 1935 this milk-bottle-opening behaviour in birds was only reported in approximately thirteen locations in the south of England, nine locations in the north-east of England and in one location on the west coast of England. However, in 1947 this behaviour was observed to occur throughout most of Britain – although the greatest activity was still occurring in the original sites. This led Fisher and Hinde to suggest that the learning of this behaviour was due to other birds observing and then imitating 'knowledgeable' birds. The original birds would have developed this behaviour possibly through trial-and-error and/or discovery learning (i.e. learning that occurs by chance due to the animal's natural curiosity and urge to explore the environment).

Experimental research as evidence for social learning in animals

Social learning in rhesus monkeys

The most elegant demonstrations of experimental evidence for observational learning are those of Darby and Riopelle (1959). In each of these experiments, two rhesus monkeys (*Macaca mulatta*) were sat facing each other across a stimulus display board. The stimulus display board was used to present the demonstrator monkey with two different objects; underneath one of these objects there was a piece of food. The demonstrator monkey was allowed to select and pick up one of the two objects in each trial. Therefore when the demonstrator monkey chooses an object and lifts it up it has a 50–50 chance of finding the food.

The observer monkey watched the demonstrator monkey on each trial and after the demonstrator monkey had made its choice the observer monkey was then given the same two objects with food hidden exactly as it was for the demonstrator monkey. If this second monkey has learned from observing the failure or success of the other monkey's choice it should pick the same object as the demonstrator monkey when it selects the object with food under it, selecting the other object when the demonstrator monkey chooses the wrong object.

The monkeys were given 1,000 trials and each trial involved completely different pairs of objects to control for association learning over the series of trials. Findings showed that the observer monkey chose the object with the food under it in over 75 per cent of the trials. Consequently, these findings show that it is not just 'monkey-see, monkey-do'. The findings show that the observer was not simply imitating the demonstrator monkey's behaviour, nor was it simply manipulating objects that it had recently observed another monkey manipulate. If this had been the case then the observer monkey would also have only had a 50–50 chance of choosing the right object, not the 75 per cent success rate that it did have.

Social learning as an explanation of milk-bottle-top opening behaviour in birds is supported by a laboratory experiment carried out by Sherry and Galef (1984). Sherry and Galef used sixteen Canadian black-backed chickadees (*Parus atricappilus*), a close relative of the British tit, in their experiment. In the first part of the study the chickadees were introduced, individually, into a cage in which an unopened milk container (like the individual portions one gets in cafés) had been placed to see if any would learn to open it. It was found that four out of the sixteen birds did learn to open the milk containers.

In the second part of the study the twelve birds that had failed to open the milk containers (learner birds) were allocated at random to one of three conditions (two experimental, one control), while the four that had learned to open the cartons were designated as 'tutor birds'. In one of the experimental conditions each of the four birds were placed in individual cages with an unopened milk container in view of a tutor bird, who was also in a cage with an unopened milk container. Thus these birds were able to observe the tutor birds opening their milk containers. In the other experimental condition the four birds were placed individually in a cage with a milk container that was already open; thus these birds had the opportunity for discovery learning. The control group involved the four birds being placed individually in a cage with an unopened milk container to give them another chance to learn to open the containers – this is trial-and-error learning. At the end the birds were all placed, individually, in a cage with an unopened milk container and were observed to see if they opened it.

Results showed that three of the learner birds in both experimental conditions now opened the milk containers, but only one of the birds in the control condition did so. They concluded that milk-bottle-top opening can be learned by observation and imitation, but that it can also be learned by discovery learning and, less successfully, by trial-and-error learning.

Evaluation of social learning in animals

Anti-behaviourists claim that social learning in animals involves cognitive processes and therefore is not simply conditional associate learning. Indeed, some anti-behaviourists, such as Köhler, go one stage further and claim that social learning implies that the animal has an understanding of the purpose of another's actions, and the imitation of these. An alternative interpretation is that these animals are merely blindly imitating the actions of others, using the simple rule of 'do as s/he does', with no understanding of the aim of the behaviour that they imitate. Support for this non-mentalistic interpretation of social learning can clearly be seen in an example given by Linden (2000). Linden cites Creswell's observation of an infant chimp that the latter was caring for. The chimp, called Ali, like many infant chimps (and humans) was prone to tantrums and in order to deal with Ali's tantrums Creswell used distraction. During one such tantrum Creswell tried to distract Ali by digging a hole in a sandpit at the back of his house. The distraction had the desired effect and Ali went over to see what Creswell was doing. Ali then proceeded to pull Creswell's hand out of the sand and sniff his fingers. Creswell just pulled his hand away and carried on digging the hole in the sand. After a few more seconds had passed Ali began digging her own hole in the sand right next to Creswell's. A few minutes later Creswell's dog wandered over to the sandpit and observed him and the chimp digging their holes for a minute or so. The dog then joined in and began digging its own hole in the sandpit. Consequently, social learning may not be as cognitively demanding as it would first appear to be.

Conclusion on social learning in animals

It can be clearly seen that social learning does occur in that animals learn from others by observing and imitating 'successful' behaviours. It can also be seen that the role of social learning does appear to be to increase an animal's fitness (i.e. the probability that it will survive long enough to get its genes into the next generation). Social learning indicates that cognition does play a role in learning in the natural environment; an indication that is damaging to behaviourists' claims that thought is simply an epiphenomenon (i.e. a useless by-product of learning). Nevertheless, the role of cognition in social learning may not be a vital factor – an animal may simply be imitating another's behaviour without any great thought at all.

Intelligence in animals

Consider the case of Fu Manchu, an orang-utan at Omaha Zoo, Nebraska who made the headlines in 1968 with his 'jail breaking' adventures. Fu Manchu and his troop had been playing in their outdoor enclosure on a sunny day, but later their shocked keepers found them playing in the trees near the elephant house – well away from their outdoor enclosure from which they had somehow escaped. Investigations revealed that the door had been left open. The supervisor, Jerry Stones, gave the staff a severe reprimand and the incident was forgotten – until, that is, they escaped again when allowed into their outdoor enclosure. Understandably Stones was looking for someone's head to roll, but before he could point the finger of blame at one of the staff he caught Fu Manchu red handed. Stones watched Fu Manchu climb down some air vent louvre doors and into a dry moat. Once in the moat he took hold of the bottom of the door, took a wire out of his mouth and used it to slip the bolt on the door back and gain freedom for himself and his troop. Stones claimed that this was the very essence of intelligent behaviour in animals – but is it?

What is intelligence?

Before we can begin to consider any evidence for intelligence in animals we must first decide what intelligence is. The term 'intelligence' has never had a universally accepted definition nor even a widely agreed definition – even with regard to human intelligence. Thus it is not surprising that whatever definition we settle upon it will not be acceptable to all. Nevertheless, we will briefly consider attempts to define intelligence and the problems related with such attempts. This will demonstrate an idea of the fundamental problems in trying to do so.

Attempts have been made to try to define intelligence in terms of mental powers or faculties such as reasoning, thinking, creativity, memory, etc. However, this is of little help because not only are these vague concepts they are also not observable, which makes research rather difficult. Further problems with definitions based on such vague concepts are confounded by the fact that intelligence is not a quantitative 'thing' like long legs or large teeth – instead, it is a 'quality' of diverse forms of behaviour.

The *Encyclopaedic Dictionary of Psychology* (Harré and Lamb, 1983) defines intelligence as 'the all round mental ability (or thinking skills) either of humans or of lower animal species'. However, this also leaves us with the problem that 'all round mental ability' or 'thinking skills' are not directly observable. Perhaps a less ambiguous way of defining intelligence is to say that it is the opposite of instinctive behaviour in that it is done with conscious intent and is reasoned, planned behaviour. This is also problematic because we then have to concede that intelligence must involve conscious thought and this may not be the case in a great deal of human 'intelligent' behaviour – for example, observational and insight learning.

Perhaps a better definition of intelligence, at least for the purpose of establishing whether animals appear to 'have it', might be gained by referring to the very behaviours that are claimed to make humans intelligent – behaviours such as tool design and use, the ability to acquire and use language, the ability to have a conscious knowledge of the world, self-awareness, and the knowledge that others may have a different perspective of the world. Put another way, an animal's behaviours that imply that it has an understanding of its world in relation to what it is trying to do, why it is doing it, what it is seeking to achieve by such actions, and the same understanding of this in others. The basis of this definition is clearly echoed in the following quote by two renowned animal researchers:

> The mixture of hormone-driven aggression, sexual and social lust for power, deceit and gamesmanship, friendship and spite, and good and ill-natured fun rings familiar chords . . . there is no reasonable way to account for much of primate [the highest order of mammals], and especially chimpanzee, behaviour without assuming that these animals understand a great deal about what they are doing and seeking to do, and are inferring almost as much as humans do about their intentions and attitudes of their peers.
>
> (Gould and Grant-Gould, 1994: 149)

Indeed Gould and Grant-Gould state that intelligence can be summed up as an 'ability to slip the bonds of instinct and generate novel solutions to problems' (1994: p. 70).

The traditional view is that intelligence is what sets humans apart from non-human animals and is typified by behaviours such as the ability to fabricate and use tools, acquire and use language, and develop a conscious awareness of their world and their self-awareness. Thus behaviourist supporters claim that only human animals have the ability to develop such behaviours and therefore, by default, only human animals have intelligence. Indeed, the traditional Skinnerian behaviourists' view of supposed non-human animal intelligence is that it does not exist. Consequently, behaviourist supporters hold that animals either do not have a conscious awareness of their world or self, or if they do it is at most an epiphenomenon (i.e. a useless by-product of brain activity).

The view portrayed in Gould and Grant-Gould's quote is in stark contrast to the traditional view of intelligence because it clearly suggests that animals do show that they have a conscious awareness of their world and the self and therefore possess intelligence. Indeed, as will be seen, animals appear to display most if not all of the very behaviours that the traditional view claims only humans are capable of acquiring.

A change from the traditional view of intelligence

Prior to the 1960s the majority of psychologists supposedly held the extreme traditional view that only humans exhibit the characteristics that constitute intelligence, but this traditional view has recently been challenged and has begun to be replaced by a new widespread view – that is, that animals have 'minds' as well as brains and therefore probably also have a conscious awareness of their world and self, at least in a limited form (Griffin, 1992), and thus *are* intelligent beings.

This 'challenge' initially came about in the early 1960s from the findings of the renowned primatologist (a person who studies **primates**) Jane Goodall who offered detailed observations of intelligent behaviour in animals.

Evidence for intelligent behaviour in animals

Goodall (1965) reported observing chimpanzees making and using tools. Very shortly after this many other researchers began to report tool fabrication and use in other animals, as well as a number of other traditionally defined intelligent behaviours. For example, when animals are faced with obstacles they have been found to show innovative, versatile adaptive responses, together with deception, intentional communication and, at least in apes, a consciousness of self and a **theory of mind**. Theory of mind is having an understanding that others possess mental states that accommodate ideas and accounts of the world that are different to their own, enabling the animal to make predictions about others' actions and motivation. Such findings suggest that, rather than animals learning by way of Skinner's somewhat inflexible 'response chain of associations', animal learning is much more innovative, versatile and highly adaptive – indeed, such highly flexible learning is frequently observed in animals, clearly implying that they do have intelligence. Some of the evidence claimed to show intelligence in animals will now be considered.

Tool fabrication and use in captive animals as evidence for intelligence

A great number of studies reporting tool fabrication and use in animals has been reported. Just a few examples will be sufficient to show evidence of this 'intelligent' behaviour.

Evidence for tool fabrication and use in captive animals

Tool fabrication and use has been observed in a number of species in captivity. Benjamin Beck reported a fascinating story on the supposed ability of a crow that lived in his laboratory. The crow was fed on dried mash that had to be moistened with water before the crow could eat it – but his keepers often forgot to do this. Nevertheless, the crow found an ingenious way of overcoming his keepers' absentmindedness. The crow had been given a plastic cup as a toy, but began to use the cup as a tool to collect water from a trough at the other side of the room, to carry it across the room and then to moisten its own food.

Goodall (1965) also observed the use of tools in captive chimpanzees. These chimpanzees had used poles in their environment to gain things that were out of their reach without them; this included freedom, as one chimp spontaneously used the pole to escape from its enclosure by 'pole vaulting' over the fence!

Linden (2000) states that tool use is more often observed in captive animals than it is in their wild counterparts. The reason for this is thought to be due to the fact that there are more opportunities to observe tool-making and using behaviour in such settings than in the animals' natural environments. Also, the captive animal has the chores of finding adequate food and water fulfilled by others, and has security from predators and protection from environmental extremes such as storm weather. As a result, it also has more time to investigate its environment than does its wild counterpart. Consequently, we cannot extrapolate findings observed in captive animals to their wild counterparts. However, tool use has also been observed in animals in the wild.

Observational evidence for tool fabrication and use in animals in the wild

As with any other area of behaviour research evidence is needed to show that animals do make and use tools. Evidence can be gained from observations of animals in their natural habitat (naturalistic observation) and observation of animals in captivity. We will now look at both sources of evidence.

TOOL FABRICATION AND USE IN WILD BIRDS

Observational research by Millikan and Bowman (1967) found that the woodpecker finch, found on the Galapagos Islands, has many talents, including tool use and fabrication. Ordinary finches have long barbed tongues that enable them to extract grubs from tree branches, but the woodpecker finch did not evolve this way and consequently is disadvantaged by its short tongue. Nevertheless, the woodpecker finch uses a cactus spine to achieve the same efficiency as ordinary finches by using it to prise grubs out of a tree branch. It was also observed that woodpecker finches adjust their posture and manipulation of the cactus tool according to its size and shape, shortening unwieldy cactus spines in order to form more manageable tools.

TOOL FABRICATION AND USE IN WILD CHIMPANZEES

As mentioned previously, Jane Goodall (1965) observed tool use in wild Tanzanian chimpanzees. They strip twigs and use them to poke into holes in termite nests to obtain this food resource without being bitten. The chimps simply poke the sticks into the termite nest, the termites act as though the nest is being attacked and climb onto the twigs, the chimps simply wait for the termites to 'board' the twigs, then pull them out and eat the termites off the twigs. Goodall has also observed these wild chimps using sticks to get honey out a beehive, to dig up edible roots, and to use them as levers to open boxes of bananas that have been left by researchers. Moreover, she has also observed them using large leaves as tools to collect and drink water from, and for wiping mud, blood and sticky fruit from their bodies.

Evaluation of tool fabrication in captive animals as evidence for intelligence

All this sounds very impressive evidence on the face of it, but some would argue that this is not really intelligent behaviour for two reasons. The first reason is that these apparently intelligent behaviours may not reflect individual problem-solving behaviour but instead simply reflect proficient imitation or social learning (Visalberghi and Fragaszy, 1992). Nevertheless, any innovative individuals could be said to be exhibiting intelligent behaviour.

The second reason is much more damaging than the first. While tool use may well involve innovative, creative problem-solving to adapt the environment to suit the animal's needs none of these tool-using and manufacturing behaviours demonstrate planned behaviour. Consider the following: no researcher has ever reported observing a woodpecker finch preparing a hoard of cactus spines for use in foraging the next day, nor chimpanzees preparing a stash of twigs ready for the following day's termite fishing.

These and many similar findings have caused many traditionalists, who claimed that tool fabrication and use was unique to humans and one of the things that set humans apart from animals, to reconsider their claim for this as evidence for a qualitative difference in human and non-human animals. Many defended their view by focusing on the two other supposedly uniquely human abilities – language and self-aware-ness, which enable the development of a theory of mind. This defence also appears to be under 'attack', as evidence for these behaviours is also apparent in non-human animals. We will only consider theory of mind here, as language in non-human animals is covered comprehensively in Nick Lund's *Animal Cognition*, another text in this series (see 'Further Reading' at the end of this chapter).

Theory of mind as evidence for intelligence in animals

A number of years have passed since Premack and Woodruff (1978) first conceptualised the theory of mind and posed the question 'Does the chimpanzee have a theory of mind?' Since that time this question has dominated the study of social behaviour in primates (as well as the study of cognitive development in human children).

What is a theory of mind?

The first things to understand about 'theory of mind' is that it is not a psychological theory like the theory of classical or operant conditioning. Theory of mind is something that must be developed in order to enable knowledge and understanding of the minds of others. It is called a theory because we can never actually directly know about another's mind, and there is no objective way to either verify the contents of another's consciousness or to assess their motivations and desires. Instead, when we interact with others we can only assume these things, using a personal theory of mind to work out what others know, think or feel.

Theory of mind can be defined as each individual animal having an understanding that others possess mental states that accommodate ideas and accounts of the world that are different to their own enabling the animal to make predictions about others' actions and motivation. The term 'theory of mind' (or ToM for short) was coined by David Premack and Guy Woodruff (1978) in a paper investigating a chimpanzee's ability to predict the behaviour of another by means of mental state attribution. Put more simply, they sought to show that their chimp, Sarah, predicted the actions of a man by deducing his 'intentions' and 'motivations' and that she reacted according to her predictions. Thus a ToM involves an understanding and knowledge that others possess mental states that contain ideas and accounts of the world that differ from one's own mental states.

In relation to the study of social behaviour in non-human primates (henceforth referred to as 'primates'), the ToM hypothesis primarily consists of claims that primates can consciously categorise and think about themselves and others. That is, they claim that primates have a conscious knowledge of the content of their mental representations of themselves and others. Some researchers use different terms to ToM; for example, Machiavellian intelligence (Byrne and Whiten, 1988), meta-cognition (Povinelli, 1995), mental state attribution (Cheyney and Seyfarth, 1992), mind reading (Whiten and Byrne, 1991), to name but a few. Nevertheless, all assert the same basic proposal – that is, they all basically claim that primates have conscious knowledge of their own mental representations about the self and others.

Six types of behaviour are said to be representative of an animal that has a theory of mind:

- imitation
- self-awareness
- social relationships
- role-taking
- deception
- perspective-taking

Evidence claiming to show that these behaviours are apparent in primates will now be considered in turn.

Imitation as evidence for ToM in primates

While imitation has already been considered earlier, it was not done with the specific purpose of establishing whether animals have a theory of mind, therefore it will be considered here with just that purpose in mind. The spontaneous copying or imitation of novel acts, referred to as motor imitation, has been regarded as a possible sign for higher intelligence in animals for a long time (e.g. Thorndike, 1898). Motor imitation is thought to show a theory of mind because it is believed that the imitator has mentally attributed purpose and/or the attainment of a goal to such behaviour. Thus imitation is said to involve conscious mental states. Motor imitation is inferred when an animal performs a complex, novel behaviour that it has seen being performed by a single individual or a succession of individuals within a social group of animals.

Many natural and controlled observations claim to show evidence of motor imitation in primates that implies they have a theory of mind – for example, in monkeys (e.g. Westergaard, 1988), in orang-utans (e.g. Russon and Galdikas, 1993) and in chimpanzees (e.g. Goodall, 1986).

Such behaviour is inferred when an animal performs a complex, novel behaviour that it has seen being performed by a single individual or a succession of individuals within a social group of animals. Indeed, the study by Kawai, cited earlier, that reported conspecifics imitating the innovative potato-washing behaviour of Imo is a prime example of a naturalistic observational study to demonstrate motor imitation. Further evidence can be gained from observations of female primates apparently purposefully teaching their offspring to imitate their use of stones to crack open nuts (Boesch, 1991).

One of the first problems with this research lies in establishing the reliability of findings gained from using an observational method. Nevertheless, even disregarding these problems the conclusion drawn from such research is not compelling. Some researchers argue that the behaviour in such studies could just as easily have been acquired by means other than motor imitation (e.g. Galef, 1992; Tomasello *et al.*, 1993), such as non-mentalistic associative learning (i.e. conditional learning); in many cases there is evidence to support this claim. For example, the claim that motor imitation was the means of learning to wash potatoes in Imo's conspecifics can be explained by non-mentalistic associative learning. Consider that when Imo, a juvenile, first exhibited this novel behaviour it then occurred in her playmates first and then in her playmates' mothers. This factor suggests that it is just as possible that each monkey may have followed or chased others (initially Imo) into the water while holding onto a sweet potato. Once in the water all each monkey had to do to acquire such behaviour was accidentally to drop the potato into the water then retrieve it in order to discover that it had resulted in a clean potato with a pleasant salty flavour (Galef, 1992; Visalberghi and Fragaszy, 1992). This was interpreted by researchers as imitation of Imo's behaviour.

While a great deal of observational research has resulted in evidence for motor imitation in primates very few experiments have been conducted to establish this, though there have been some. Hayes and Hayes (1952) carried out an experiment on their chimpanzee Viki. They exposed Viki to seventy 'imitation set' tasks. Each task consisted of the experimenter saying to Viki 'Do this' and then performing an action, for example operating a toy or patting his head. Hayes and Hayes claimed that Viki showed motor imitation in over fifty of the seventy imitation set tasks, ten of which involved completely novel, arbitrary actions. Thus they concluded that this was clear evidence for motor imitation in a primate.

To overcome such criticisms Custance *et al.* (1995) carried out a careful replication of the Hayes and Hayes procedure using two young human-reared, language-trained chimpanzees and a means of measuring the degree of similarity between the chimpanzees' and the experimenter's actions. After using shaping to get the chimpanzees to imitate fifteen actions performed by the experimenter on the command of 'Do this' they presented them with a further forty-eight novel 'Do this' commands without giving a reward. Results showed that while the chimpanzees successfully imitated thirteen of the fifteen initial 'Do this' command actions with a high level of similarity, they only successfully imitated seventeen of the forty-eight novel 'Do this' command actions – and with a lesser degree of similarity. This study initially appears to provide evidence that chimpanzee primates do exhibit motor imitation, consequently offering support for the mentalistic claim for a theory of mind in primates. This conclusion is wrong, however, because such training is not necessary in the wild, consequently it is not representative of an animal's behaviour in its natural setting and therefore lacks **external (ecological) validity**.

EVALUATION OF IMITATION AS EVIDENCE FOR TOM IN PRIMATES

While the above study is probably the strongest evidence to show that chimpanzee primates exhibit imitation, this supposed imitation behaviour could just as easily be explained by non-mentalistic means. The pair of chimps may simply have been engaging in matched-dependent behaviour; that is, copying the experimenter's behaviour because they had learned that doing so resulted in a pleasant outcome (e.g. a smile from the experimenter) without being consciously aware that their behaviour was similar to the experimenter's. Since humans raised both chimpanzees they would have been used to playing imitation games and receiving smiles and cuddles for doing so. Consequently, the possibility that these chimpanzees had been rewarded for imitative behaviour before the experiment cannot be ruled out; neither can the fact that they may have simply generalised their behaviour from the initial training sessions. Thus these non-mentalistic explanations are just as viable as the mentalistic claims for conscious imitation.

Not surprisingly the conclusion to date is that it is not clear whether apes or any other primates can 'ape' (that is, imitate). Nor whether imitation involves the imitator representing the demonstrator's mental state, point of view, and a knowledge of what and why they are imitating the demonstrator's behaviour (Tomasello, 1996). In addition, it is argued that a capacity to imitate another is not a valid means of establishing whether non-human primates have a ToM. This is mainly because any imitation performed by an animal must occur without any training or tuition to ensure that the animal *is* imitating the demonstrator's behaviour and has not simply learned to do what the demonstrator *wants* the animal to do. Unfortunately, it appears to be the case that most animals trained in imitation are simply doing what the demonstrator *wants* them to do (Heyes, 1998) and are not exhibiting true imitative behaviour. There is no valid experimental evidence to date that shows imitation in animals occurring without training, therefore it may be better to look elsewhere for evidence for a theory of mind in such animals.

Self-awareness as evidence for ToM in animals

Self-awareness is a precursor for the development of a theory of mind. It refers to consciousness of the self as a separate individual and occupies the next level above conscious awareness of events and objects in the world. Self-awareness therefore implies that an animal has developed a self-concept; this should be shown in its ability to recognise itself. Of course, such levels of consciousness can only ever be inferred and not directly observed and this must always be kept in mind when considering evidence for these behaviours.

RESEARCH ON SELF-AWARENESS IN ANIMALS

Research has shown that many animals do not appear to have developed self-awareness because many seem unable to recognise themselves. For example, when animals such as parakeets and Siamese fighting fish see an image of themselves in a mirror they treat it as if it were another conspecific, often attacking the image ferociously. Thus such animals do not appear to recognise themselves at all. Cats and dogs, on the other hand, stare at the mirror image for a while and then simply ignore it, again suggesting a lack of self-recognition and a lack of a self-concept. Research has shown, though, that the chimpanzee, our closest evolutionary relative, does appear to develop a self-concept.

Observational research carried out by de Waal (1989) has shown that when chimpanzees inspect their image in a mirror they initially treat the image as though it is another animal. However, after a few days they appear to have realised that it is their own image. Now they begin to appear to show self-directed behaviour, such as using the mirror to groom themselves, giving the impression that they have an idea of what their appearance should be like. They cover their bodies with objects (for example, they put bananas on their head); they also use the mirror to inspect areas of their bodies that would otherwise be inaccessible (e.g. Cheyney and Seyfarth, 1990; Jolly, 1991). Thus it appears that they have self-recognition and therefore must have self-awareness.

Observational evidence like that cited above is very weak and it may be possible to gain stronger evidence from experimental research. A series of experiments have used the mirror-test and claimed to show that chimpanzees and orang-utans are capable of developing a self-awareness, but that other primates or non-primate animals are not (e.g. Povinelli, 1995; Gallup, 1977). The mirror-test procedure, originally developed by Gallup, involves anaesthetising an animal that has previously had some experience of observing its image in a mirror. Once the animal is under the influence of the anaesthetic the researcher applies a dot of odourless, non-irritating dye to its forehead. When the animal gains consciousness it is observed in order to establish how many times it touches the mark on its forehead – first in the absence of a mirror and then in the presence of a mirror. The reasoning behind such studies is that if an animal does have self-awareness then it will touch the mark on its forehead significantly more when looking at its image in a mirror than in the absence of a mirror.

Results of such studies reliably show that chimpanzees and orang-utans do indeed touch the marks on their foreheads much more when they can see their images in a mirror than when they cannot. However, other primates and non-primate animals exhibit very low levels of touching the marks on their foreheads in both the mirror-absent and mirror-present conditions.

This experimental evidence is claimed by mentalistic advocates to imply that chimpanzees and orang-utans (at least) have self-awareness, including the ability to visualise how others view them, and consequently assert that such animals have a rudimentary theory of mind. Heyes (1998) offers an alternative non-mentalistic interpretation of these findings.

AN EVALUATION OF SELF-AWARENESS AS EVIDENCE FOR TOM IN ANIMALS

Heyes asserts that the reason for chimpanzees' and orang-utans' greater mark-touching behaviour in these experiments is due to the fact that chimpanzees and orang-utans exhibit much more head touching in the wild than any other primates species do (Gallup *et al.*, 1995). Therefore it is, she claims, a naturally occurring phenomenon and possibly nothing to do with self-awareness. Moreover, she claims that the reason why chimpanzees and orang-utans touch the marks much more in the mirror-present condition than they do in the mirror-absent condition is due to what she terms 'the anaesthetic artefact hypothesis'. This hypothesis asserts that because the mirror-present condition always comes quite a long time after the mirror-absent condition in these studies it means that the primates are much more active and alert in this condition and that this is therefore a serious confounding variable.

Nevertheless there are problems for the anaesthetic artefact hypothesis; it could quite easily be ruled out as a valid explanation by conducting a simple study. One could compare the frequency that these animals touch unmarked areas of the body as well as marked areas in both conditions. Thus if they touched unmarked areas as frequently in the mirror-absent and the mirror-present conditions it could not be due to the effects of the anaesthetic, hence ruling out this hypothesis. De Veer and van den Bos (1999) have carried a number of such studies and their findings show that chimpanzees and orang-utans did indeed touch unmarked areas as frequently in the mirror-absent and the mirror-present conditions. Therefore such behaviour is not, as Heyes claims, due to the effects of the anaesthetic; hence these findings appear to rule out this hypothesis. In conclusion, these animals may have self-awareness and, consequently, a theory of mind.

Social relationships as evidence for a ToM in animals

There is a substantial and growing body of evidence that suggests that the social behaviour of primates is affected by much more than interactions with other individual conspecifics. For example, it has been found that the social behaviour of primates is affected by the outcome of previous interactions with other individual conspecifics and by the individual's observations of others animals' social interactions. Thus, for example, animal A's behaviour towards animal B is not only affected by its present and previous interactions with animal B but also by its observations of animal B's present and previous interactions with conspecifics other than itself. As a result, such social behaviour has been forwarded as evidence that these animals have a theory of mind. Such a claim logically follows, as it is proposed that such social relationships involve knowledge of one's own intentions as well as knowledge of others' – both represented in mental states. Evidence for such social relationships has been derived from observational and experimental research involving a variety of primate species. One example will suffice to make the point.

Stammbach (1988) carried out a field experiment to determine whether long-tailed monkeys exhibited social relationships. This involved training one subordinate monkey from each troop to obtain preferred food by manipulating three levers and then to share the food with other monkeys in the troop. Stammbach found that the other monkeys in the troop did not imitate the lever-manipulating monkey's behaviour, although they did begin to follow it to the lever apparatus where they spent increasing amounts of time sitting beside and grooming the lever-manipulating monkey. Stammbach and Kummer (1990) interpreted this behaviour as being caused by the fact that the untrained monkeys had acquired knowledge that the lever-manipulating monkey had superior knowledge of how to obtain preferred food than they did. Consequently they spent increasingly more time following, sitting with and grooming the trained monkey because they wanted to develop friendly social relations with it to increase the probability that it would give them some of the preferred food.

Stammbach and Kummer's interpretation smacks of anthropomorphism (i.e. attributing human qualities to animals). Moreover, such findings could just as easily be explained by non-mentalistic associative learning; that is, being near to the trained animal had become associated with the receipt of preferred food and consequently the acts of following, sitting near and grooming this animal were reinforced by the receipt of the food.

EVALUATION OF SOCIAL RELATIONSHIPS AS EVIDENCE FOR TOM IN ANIMALS

In conclusion, both mentalistically and non-mentalistically oriented researchers agree with the argument that animals (in particular primates) have knowledge of social relationships. Where they differ is on their views about the type of knowledge these animals have about social relationships. The mentalistically oriented researchers claim that some primates have knowledge of the social relationships that are represented in mental states, thus positing that they have a theory of mind. However, non-mentalistically oriented researchers claim that such animals simply have knowledge about basic associations gained from observing their own and their conspecifics' interactions. It would appear that the latter claim is the most probable, if only on the grounds of it being less generous. Therefore the overall present conclusion is that animals probably only have knowledge about basic associations gained from observing their own and their conspecifics, consequently weakening the claim that animals have a theory of mind.

Role-taking as evidence for ToM in animals

Role-taking is the process of being able mentally to put oneself in the place of others. It is thought to show a theory of mind because it requires the role-taker to have the knowledge that others have mental states, and therefore the cognisance, to attribute others with beliefs, desires, intentions, etc., that may be different or similar to one's own.

It was Premack and Woodruff's (1978) experiments with the language-trained chimpanzee, Sarah, that led them to develop the theory of mind supposition and to pose the questions on whether chimpanzees did have a theory of mind. During these experiments, devised to show whether Sarah understood the language she had acquired, they showed Sarah videotapes of human actors attempting to solve different problems – for example, attempting to escape from a locked cage or trying to obtain out-of-reach food. Just before the film showed whether the actors were successful or unsuccessful in their attempts to solve the problems the video was put on hold. Sarah was then given a choice of one of two photographs, the first depicting the actor performing an action that would result in a solution to the problem and the other an action that would not result in a solution.

Sarah consistently selected the photograph that depicted the actor performing an action that would lead to the correct solution to the problem. These findings led Premack and Woodruff to conclude that this was clear evidence that Sarah had attributed mental states to the actors and, further, to the conclusion that she had a theory of mind. They reasoned that if Sarah had not attributed beliefs, desires, intentions, etc. to the actor in each video she could not have selected the photograph depicting the correct solution to the problem. This is because had she not attributed mental states to the actors she would simply have perceived the videotapes and the photograph choices as an undifferentiated sequence of events and not as a problem-solving situation.

EVALUATION OF ROLE-TAKING AS EVIDENCE FOR TOM IN ANIMALS

Unlike the evidence previously considered for a ToM in animals this is not as readily dismissed by a non-mentalistic explanation. Nevertheless, a non-mentalistic explanation of Sarah's correct choice is possible. For example, Sarah's success could have been due to physical matching; that is, she used physical cues in the video and photographs to enable her to match them, or previously learned associations and/or familiarity with a given situation. Consider that in the video depicting the actor trying to obtain out-of-reach food there was a long stick lying horizontally, and that this stick was also prominent in one of the two photographs but not the other. In such a case Sarah could simply match these physical cues to reach what appeared to be a correct choice.

Povinelli *et al.* (1992) have shown that pairs of chimpanzees can reverse roles after being trained to perform complementary parts of a single task. This experiment involved ensuring that one chimpanzee was able to see where food was located but could not reach it, whereas the other chimpanzee was unable to see where the food was located but was in a position to reach it. They trained the chimpanzee that could see the food to guide the chimpanzee that could not see it to obtain the food. Once the chimpanzees had learned how to do this task the roles were reversed. This was done to see if the chimpanzee who had previously been unable to see the food, but could now see it, would know that the other chimpanzee could not see the food but could reach it and vice versa. Results showed that the chimpanzees were able to reverse roles immediately, clearly providing strong evidence that each chimpanzee had acquired knowledge of the other chimpanzee's perspective and that it was different to their own.

In conclusion, role-taking appears to be the most promising support for a theory of mind in animals. Therefore the answer to our main question, 'are animals intelligent?', is yes – at least in the species considered.

Deception as evidence for ToM in animals

Consider the following observation by Helen Shewman, a zoo keeper at Seattle's Woodland Park Zoo. Shewman stated that she placed an orange through a feeding hole, as is usual, for a female orang-utan named Melati. However, instead of moving away, as she normally did, Melati looked Shewman straight in the eye and held out her hand. Thinking that the first orange must have rolled away out of Melati's reach Shewman placed another orange in the orang-utan's outstretched hand; however, as Melati wandered off, Shewman realised that she had been hiding the first orange behind her back in her other hand. Towan, the dominant male in Melati's group, had watched this whole charade and the very next day looked Shewman straight in the eye after she had given him his orange and held out his empty hand. When Shewman asked Towan 'Are you sure you don't already have one?', Towan steadfastly stared at her at the same time as beckoning her to give him another orange. On relenting, Shewman found that Towan had been hiding the first orange under his foot – double deception or what? (see Linden, 2000).

The use of deception is a strong contender for showing that animals have a theory of mind. This is because if an animal intentionally deceives another it clearly implies that the deceiver has knowledge of another's mental states (beliefs, desires, intentions, etc.), as well as knowledge of the consequences of such deceit. However, before considering evidence for deception in animals it should be pointed out that while there are two main uses of the term 'deception' in animal research only one of these uses is valid in relation to establishing whether animals have a theory of mind. One use of the term 'deception' is a functional use, referring to one animal leading another to make an incorrect or inappropriate response due to another animal's suppression or production of behaviour. For example, when the plover bird acts as if it has a broken wing to lead a predator away from its young (Ristau, 1991) it serves the function of deceiving the predator by portraying itself as 'easy prey', but when the predator gets near it simply flies to safety. There are vast amounts of research to show examples of functional deception, but such acts do not require an animal to have a theory of mind and can be readily explained by a non-mentalistic approach. On the other hand *intentional* deception, the other use of the term, does require a theory of mind and is not readily explained by a non-mentalistic approach; hence it is evidence for this type of deception that will be considered here.

Strum (cited by Jolly, 1988) reported observing a female baboon intentionally deceiving a male baboon. It is the male baboon who normally does most of the hunting for meat and when he has caught his prey he is unwilling to share it with a female, only allowing her access to the carcass when he has had enough to eat. However, one of the females in the troop observed by Strum had become very fond of meat and it appeared that she was not prepared to wait for the meagre pickings left by a male. She approached a male baboon that had just caught and killed an antelope and started to groom him. Her grooming made the male relax and drop into a reclining position, whereupon it released its grasp on the carcass; the female then seized the antelope carcass and ran. Strum claims this is clear evidence for intentional deception and hence a theory of mind.

Nevertheless, such behaviour can also be explained just as readily by a non-mentalistic account. This female could have learned via association. In the past she could have attempted to snatch food from other conspecifics without initially paying any attention to their body posture, eventually learning through experience that she is much more successful at snatching food when the conspecific is in a reclined position. Thus as she groomed the male with the carcass she realised that he was in a reclined position and simply snatched the carcass. Consequently, the snatching of the carcass from this male may have been an automatic response to an animal in a relaxed position, rather than a planned and intentional response. Again, hardly strong evidence to support the theory of mind advocates.

Over a decade later Whiten and Byrne (1991) took a different approach to addressing whether primates show evidence of intentional deception, and hence a theory of mind. Having observed what appeared to be intentional deception in their own studies of primates, and being told by so many other researchers of incidences of apparent intentional deception, they became convinced that these incidences were too numerous for there not to be a grain of truth in them. Inspired by this belief Whiten and Byrne set about painstakingly compiling records of examples of such evidence in the hope of convincing others that humans are not the only animals to use intentional deception. This culminated in a catalogue of evidence of intentional deception in primates which by 1990 involved over 250 individual observations of such behaviour. Examples of deception observed include the following. Infidelity involving female primates hiding from dominant males and suppressing their usual copulation calls (presumably to avoid violent reprisals from the dominant male) whilst mating with a subordinate male. Subservient males taking turns to distract the dominant male with threats of aggression while the other mates with one of his females – and then reversing their roles. Observation of a vervet monkey that had angered a conspecific. The conspecific had cornered the vervet monkey, upon which it proceeded to deceive the conspecific by looking into the trees and giving the 'predator approaching' call. This deceiving alarm call caused the pursuing conspecific to divert his attention to finding the supposed predator and ended the aggressive pursuit of the monkey that had angered the conspecific.

EVALUATION OF DECEPTION AS EVIDENCE FOR TOM IN ANIMALS

Despite the impressive quantity of Whiten and Byrne's evidence it has to be conceded that it is still only anecdotal, and can never prove involvement in intentional deception. Nevertheless, the authors 'stick to their guns' in their belief that, at least as far as great apes are concerned, this data points to a real theory of mind. Therefore the answer to our main question 'are animals intelligent?' appears to be yes – at least those species studied by Whiten and Byrne.

Unfortunately this belief may be misplaced, especially in the light of contradictory research findings in perspective-taking, covered next, which show that primates, including the great apes, fail the Sally–Anne test used to show that children have a theory of mind. Consequently, a conclusion on whether animals intentionally deceive others will be postponed until such evidence has been considered.

Perspective-taking as evidence for ToM in animals

Consider the following observation by Charlene Jendry, a primate conservationist at Columbus Zoo in Ohio. Jendry was called to the zoo because Colo, a female gorilla, was reported to be clutching a suspicious object and, as the zoo keeper had been unable to find out what it was, they were concerned for Colo and for her troop's safety. When Jendry arrived at Colo's enclosure she approached her and offered her some peanuts, but Colo simply responded by giving Jendry a blank stare. Jendry states that she suddenly realised that Colo was negotiating with her and upped her offer to some peanuts and a piece of pineapple. Colo is reported to have maintained eye contact with Jendry as she opened her hand to reveal a key chain and, on seeing it was not dangerous, Jendry gave Colo the food she had offered. Colo then broke the chain and gave Jendry a link for the negotiated food – perhaps Colo realised that she could negotiate more food for each link rather than giving Jendry the whole chain. Thus it would appear that Colo had knowledge that her perspective was different to Jendry's (see Linden, 2000).

Perspective-taking is said to involve a theory of mind because it is claimed to require knowledge that one individual has a different perspective to another and thus requires mental concepts of the self and others. Consequently, if it can be shown that animals do appear to have knowledge that another's perspective is different to their own, this should be shown in their responses – precisely what the Sally–Anne test is designed to show in children.

THE SALLY–ANNE TEST

The Sally–Anne test (Baron-Cohen *et al.* 1985) involves an observer (usually a child) watching two dolls, one named Sally and the other one Anne. A researcher manipulates the 'Sally' doll so that it appears to be putting a marble into a basket and then leaving the room. When Sally has left the room a second researcher manipulates the 'Anne' doll so that it enters the room and moves the marble from the basket and places it in a box. When this is complete the observer is asked where Sally will look for the marble when she returns. Thus it follows that, if the observer realises that Sally does not have the same knowledge as they have – because Sally was not present to see Anne moving the marble to the box, they should answer 'in the basket'. Such respondents will therefore be exhibiting perspective-taking behaviour and are therefore said to possess a theory of mind. However, if the observer fails to conclude that Sally's perspective is different to theirs they will state that she will look in the box; consequently they are not exhibiting perspective-taking behaviour and are said not to have a theory of mind.

Research using humans has shown that, typically, children under the age of four years do not realise that Sally does not have the knowledge that the marble has been moved and when asked where Sally will look they answer 'in the box'. This suggests that they have not developed the skill of perspective-taking yet and therefore have not developed a theory of mind. However, children over four years old do appear to realise that Sally cannot have the knowledge that the marble has been moved and when asked where Sally will look they answer 'in the basket'.

Research using the Sally–Anne test on language-taught primates (mainly chimpanzees) aged between five and six years has shown that none passed the test (Tomasello and Call, 1994). This finding leaves us with the problem of reconciling these findings with Whiten and Byrne's vast amount of evidence for intentional deception in animals, because intentional deception implies perspective-taking. Marc Hauser believes he has the answer to this dilemma in that he attributes primates' failure on the Sally–Anne test to the flawed methodology of these studies. Hauser points out that it is grossly inappropriate to test for evidence of a theory of mind in non-human primates using a test that has been specifically designed to test for this in humans. To overcome this objection Hauser has devised an 'ape version' of the Sally–Anne test, which he has used to test for a theory of mind in cotton-top tamarin monkeys and pre-verbal human children (under two years of age).

AN APE VERSION OF THE SALLY–ANNE TEST

Hauser's (1988) 'ape version' of the Sally–Anne test involves an individual monkey observing an actor watching where an object is hidden. When the object has been hidden a screen is raised to prevent the actor seeing another person move the object to a different location but does not prevent the monkey from seeing where the object is relocated. The screen is then removed and the actor either looks in the new location or the old location. Hauser reasoned that if an individual was aware that the actor could not know about the new location they should respond differently when they observe the actor looking in the new location and the old location. Hauser further reasoned that if an actor looks in the new location an observer with a theory of mind should spend more time staring at the actor who looks in the new location rather than at the actor who looks in the old location. This is because the former violates the observer's knowledge that the actor cannot know the new location due to s/he not seeing the object being moved.

Results showed that both monkeys and pre-verbal children stare significantly longer when the actor looks in the new location than when the actor looks in the old location. Consequently, Hauser claims that this is clear evidence that these monkeys do know that the actor has a different perspective to them and therefore that they have a theory of mind. Hauser also claims that pre-verbal children have a theory of mind and that the reason why children under four years old fail the Sally–Anne test is because they are not verbally proficient enough to express perspective knowledge, rather than that they are not able to know that others have a different perspective.

Progress exercise

A researcher places a sweet into a tin on the table and then leaves the room. A second researcher takes the sweet from the tin, puts the tin back on the table, and places the sweet in his pocket and then sits down next to the tin. Imagine that a chimpanzee has observed these actions.

If the chimpanzee has a ToM then where should it expect the returning researcher to look for the sweet? And if it does not have a ToM where should it expect the returning researcher to look for the sweet?

EVALUATION OF PERSPECTIVE-TAKING AS EVIDENCE FOR TOM IN ANIMALS

As we have seen, the findings gained from research using five- to six-year-old primates (mainly chimpanzees) show that these animals are not capable of perspective-taking when using the traditional Sally–Anne test as a measure. Some psychologists, such as Povinelli and Eddy (1996), suggest that the reason these studies failed to show perspective-taking in these animals is due to their age. This appears to be a reasonable suggestion as other research, using humans, has shown that maturation and experience play a vital role in human development of ToM. Nevertheless, while research using the ape version of the Sally–Anne test does show that apes are capable of perspective-taking, it could be argued that it may not be measuring the same thing as the traditional Sally–Anne test, consequently weakening the evidence for perspective-taking abilities in animals. To date the overall conclusion must be that there is no incontestable evidence that animals are able to have an understanding of another's perspective; therefore the non-mentalistic approach appears to be supported, if only by default.

Overall conclusion on evidence for theory of mind in animals

Research on imitation and self-awareness implies that animals do not have a theory of mind and that the most plausible explanation for such behaviour is probably non-mentalistic (i.e. conditional learning via classical and operant conditioning). In terms of social relations we must conclude that animals probably only have a very basic understanding, again supporting the non-mentalistic approach. With reference to evidence for role-taking behaviour in primates it is not so easy to dismiss the mentalistic explanation, as Sarah's competence at matching problem-solution images is difficult, if not impossible, to explain using a non-mentalistic account. While there is little doubt that research has shown that primates (at least) do exhibit deception, what is not clear is whether such use is intentional. It would appear that the less generous non-mentalistic explanation could account for such behaviour equally as well as a mentalistic explanation. Finally, in relation to evidence for perspective-taking behaviour in animals, the evidence remains inconclusive. To date, therefore, the overall conclusion must be that there is no incontestable evidence that animals do have a theory of mind. Thus the non-mentalistic approach appears to be supported, if only by default.

On a more positive note, one of the major criticisms of research that attempts to show intelligence in animals is that if animals really have intelligence then they will exhibit this best when it serves their own purpose – rather than when the researchers expect them to! The quote below from Sue Savage-Rumbaugh (1994), the renowned primatologist, is probably the most appropriate way to end this chapter:

> The apes I know behave every living, breathing moment as though they have minds that are very much like my own. They

may not think about as many things, or in the depth that I do, and they may not plan ahead as I do. Apes . . . make tools and co-ordinate their actions during the hunting of prey. But no ape has been observed to plan far enough ahead to combine the skills of tool construction and hunting for a common purpose. Such activities were a prime factor in the lives of early hominids. These greater skills that I have as a human being are the reason that I am able to construct my own shelter, earn my own salary, and follow written laws. They allow me to behave as a civilised person but they do not mean that I think while apes merely react.

(Savage-Rumbaugh, 1994: 260)

Summary

Social learning in animals that live in groups is highly adaptive because it means that animals are given far more opportunities for learning than are those who live a solitary existence. There is a great deal of evidence for social learning in animals which clearly shows that learning is much more complex and varied than the non-mentalistic theorists would suggest. There is also evidence for intelligence in animals in the form of learning to manufacture and use tools. In the time since Premack and Woodruff (1978) first asked 'Does the chimpanzee have a theory of mind?' researchers working with non-human primates have sought to evaluate the presence or absence of intelligence denoted by abilities considered to be essential to a theory of mind. Investigators seeking to uncover the nature and evolution of primate intelligence have researched imitation, self-awareness, social relationships, role-taking, deception, and perspective-taking. While there is evidence that some primates may have developed a theory of mind, this evidence, at least to date, remains inconclusive and much more research is required to come to a clear judgement on this question. This is because the basic component of a theory of mind is undoubtedly the ability to attribute mental states to others. In other words, an individual who possesses a theory of mind is capable of reasoning of the following type: 'X thinks Y' or 'A believes B'; to date, this has not been reliably seen in non-human animals.

Further reading

Byrne, R. W. and Whiten, A. (eds) (1988) *Machiavellian Intelligence*, Oxford: Oxford University Press. An excellent coverage of social learning in animals and the debate on whether animals' behaviour is intelligent.

Griffin, D. (1992) *Animal Minds*, Chicago: University of Chicago Press.

Linden, E. (2000) *The Parrot's Lament*, London: Souvenir Press. A highly readable and up-to-date account of intelligence in animals with some very amusing observations of animal behaviour.

Lund, N. (2002) *Animal Cognition*, Hove: Routledge. An accessible and well-illustrated account of this area of comparative psychology.

Slater, P. J. B., Rosenblatt, J. S., Beer, C. and Milinski, M. (eds) (1996) *Advances in the Study of Behaviour*, San Diego, Calif.: Academic Press. This text, and the one by Griffin (1992), is very readable on the evidence for social learning and for the debate on intelligence in animals.

5

Study skills

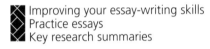

Improving your essay-writing skills
Practice essays
Key research summaries

Improving your essay-writing skills

At this point in the book you have acquired the knowledge necessary to tackle the exam itself. Answering exam questions is a skill that this chapter shows you how to improve. Examiners obviously have first-hand knowledge about what goes wrong in exams. For example, candidates frequently do not answer the question which has been set; rather, they answer the one that they hoped would come up, or they do not make effective use of the knowledge they have but just 'dump their psychology' on the page and hope the examiner will sort it out for them. A grade 'C' answer usually contains appropriate material but tends to be limited in detail and commentary. To lift such an answer to a grade 'A' or 'B' may require no more than a little more detail, better use of material and coherent organisation. It is important to appreciate it may not involve writing at any greater length, but might even necessitate the elimination of passages which do not add to the quality of the answer and some elaboration of those which do.

By studying the essays presented in this chapter, and the examiner's comments, you can learn how to turn your grade 'C' into a grade 'A'.

Typically, it only involves an extra 4 marks out of 24. Please note that marks given by the examiner in the practice essays should be used as a guide only and are not definitive. They represent the 'raw' marks which would be likely to be given to answers to AQA(A) questions. In the AQA(A) examination, an examiner would award a maximum of 12 marks for knowledge and understanding (called Assessment Objective 1 – AO1) and 12 marks for evaluation, analysis and commentary (Assessment Objective 2 – AO2). The details of this marking scheme are given in Appendix C of Paul Humphreys' title in this series, *Exam Success in AEB Psychology*, and in his forthcoming title *Exam Success in AQA(A) Psychology*. Remember that these are the raw marks and not the same as those given on the examination certificate received ultimately by the candidate, because all examining boards are required to use a common standardised system – the Uniform Mark Scale (UMS) – which adjusts all raw scores to a single standard across all boards.

The essays given here are ones that, hypothetically, could be written by an eighteen-year-old in 35–40 minutes (leaving extra time for planning and checking through your answer), and these questions would be marked bearing this in mind. It is important when writing to such a tight time limit that you make every sentence count. Each essay in this chapter is followed by detailed comments about its strengths and weaknesses. The most common problems to watch out for are:

- Failure to answer the question but reproducing a model answer to a similar question that you have pre-learned.
- Not delivering the right balance between description (assessment objective 1) and evaluation/analysis (assessment objective 2). Remember they are always weighted 50/50.
- Writing 'everything you know' about a topic in the hope that something will get credit and the examiner will sort your work out for you. Remember that excellence demands selectivity, so removing material that is irrelevant to the question set and elaborating material that is relevant can often make improvements.
- Failing to use your material effectively. It is not enough to place the information on the page; you must also show the examiner that you are using it to make a particular point.

For more ideas on how to write good essays you should consult *Exam Success in AEB Psychology* and the forthcoming title *Exam Success in AQA(A) Psychology* (both by Paul Humphreys) in this series.

Practice essay 1

*(a) Outline the nature of classical and operant conditioning.
(12 marks)*
*(b) Evaluate the role of either classical or operant conditioning.
(12 marks)*

Starting point: This two-part question should be addressed clearly by answering part (a) and part (b) separately.

Part (a): 'Outline' means state the important features of whatever it is you are being asked to outline. In this case it is the features of classical and operant conditioning. This part of the question is relatively straightforward and requires you to show knowledge and understanding of the main features of classical and operant conditioning. Consequently, this part of the question involves assessment objective 1: Therefore you are required to give a summary description only.

Part (b): The second part of the question requires that you consider whether classical or operant conditioning plays a role in non-human animal behaviour and, if it does, to what extent does it play a role. Therefore this part of the question involves assessment objective 2.

Candidate's answer

Part (a): Classical conditioning and operant conditioning are both explanations of learning.

Classical conditioning is a form of learning involving involuntary responses. The way it works is by pairing an unconditional stimulus with a conditional stimulus and after a number of pairings these stimuli become associated in such a way that when the conditional stimulus is presented without the unconditional stimulus it results in a response that was previously only elicited by the unconditional stimulus. It is also known as Pavlovian conditioning.

Operant conditioning is a form of learning in which voluntary behaviour becomes more or less likely to be repeated, depending on its consequences. It is also known as Skinnerian or instrumental conditioning. The way operant conditioning works is on the basis of the consequences of an animal performing a voluntary response. The consequences can be good or bad in that these can be in the form of either a reward or the end of something pleasant. These consequences are known as 'reinforcers' because they reinforce the likelihood that a response will or will not be performed in the future.

The most important feature of operant conditioning is therefore reinforcement that can be either negative or positive. Negative reinforcement refers to unpleasant consequences and positive reinforcement refers to pleasant consequences. Positive reinforcement leads to an increase in the likelihood that animals will perform the response in the future and negative reinforcement leads to a decrease in the likelihood that an animal will perform the response in the future.

Examiner's comments

This essay clearly addresses the question set as s/he does outline some of the main features of both classical and operant conditioning; however, it suffers from two weaknesses. Its first weakness is due to an uneven coverage of both types of conditioning – that is, the writer only outlines one main factor in classical conditioning and outlines a number of the main factors in operant conditioning. The second weakness is its failure to outline most of the main factors in both types of conditioning. Consequently, this part of the question could have been improved by offering more of the main features of classical conditioning (e.g. the associations made between an involuntary behaviour and a conditional stimulus) and operant conditioning (e.g. schedules of reinforcement). The final mark for this part of the question is likely to be about 5/6 marks.

Candidate's answer

Part (b): Operant conditioning has clearly been shown to play a role in the behaviour of non-human animals. For example, Skinner's experiments on laboratory animals under controlled conditions have shown that operant conditioning plays a role in the behaviour of these animals. A study has shown that operant conditioning does play a role in the behaviour of wild snow monkeys, because when researchers left food on the beach for them they quickly learned that if they went to the beach it would result in a positive outcome – that is, they would receive a 'free meal'.

While research has shown that operant conditioning does play a role in animal behaviour it appears that it only plays a small role. It is now believed that there are many other factors involved in animal behaviour, such as genetic inheritance, cognitive factors and social learning – that is, watching others.

It has been found that some animal behaviour is due to genetic inheritance, such as pecking behaviour. For example, research has shown that tits peck at objects in their environment due to genetic inheritance and this may lead them to learn that pecking at a milk bottle top can lead to food.

Research has shown that a great deal of animal behaviour is due to social learning, whereby an animal observes another animal's response and the consequences of this. If the consequences are good the observer animal may copy the behaviour of the observed animal, but if the consequences are bad it may not. For example, one of the snow monkeys in the study already mentioned took her sweet potato down to the sea and washed the mud off it. Shortly after this many of the other monkeys in the group did the same.

In conclusion it would appear that operant conditioning does appear to play a role in the behaviour of non-human animals, but it does not appear to play a major role.

Examiner's comments

The writer has provided a lively and straight-to-the-point answer for this part of the question and then offers research evidence in support of his/her claim. Nevertheless, by stating 'A study has shown that operant conditioning does play a role in the behaviour of wild snow monkeys' the writer gives the impression that s/he does not know who did the study or where it was done. Moreover, detail about the study is somewhat sparse and more detail (i.e. more depth of knowledge) should improve the mark. Also, while the writer does link the findings of the study 'they quickly learned that if they went to the beach it would result in a positive outcome – that is, they would receive a "free meal"' it is not explained how and/or why this is an example of operant conditioning; such an explanation would improve the grade. The writer also offers very little evidence for the role of operant conditioning in the behaviour of non-human animals, and consequently more coverage of this (i.e. more breadth of knowledge) should improve the grade.

The writer has used research findings to evaluate the extent of the role that operant conditioning plays in the behaviour of non-human animals well. Nevertheless, again the studies used in the evaluation lack detail. As previously stated, the grade of the essay could be improved by offering more detail (depth of knowledge). The final mark for this part of the question is likely to be about 8/9 marks. Together with the 5/6 marks gained in the first part this gives a total of 13/15 marks – a good grade C.

Practice question 2

'The only difference between human and non-human animals is that humans have intelligence while non-human animals do not.' *Discuss evidence for intelligence in non-human animals. (24 marks)*

Starting point: 'Discuss' is a term that requires you to present your knowledge and understanding of evidence for intelligence in non-human animals and to also evaluate your chosen evidence.

One of the problems with a question such as this is that there is so much that you could include, which may result in writing in too much breadth and in the sacrifice of detail (i.e. failure to show depth).

Note that this question does not require you to address the quote in your answer; it is there merely to stimulate thinking. What the question does ask of you is that you discuss evidence. This should be considered in terms of how it shows intelligence in non-human animals and should point out any weaknesses, methodological or otherwise, in the evidence presented.

Candidate's answer

The main sources of evidence for intelligence in non-human animals come from research that shows that they can generate novel solutions to problems that are beyond the realms of instinctual behaviour. Such evidence can be seen in non-human animal tool manufacture and use; there is also evidence that indicates that they have a theory of mind (ToM).

Research has also shown that non-human animals have a ToM that is accepted as evidence for intelligence in humans and therefore should be accepted as intelligence in non-human animals. ToM is something that must be developed to enable animals to have the knowledge and understanding that themselves and others possess ideas and internal accounts of the world and 'knowing' that in others these may be different to their own.

Examiner's comments

Writer offers evidence of knowledge regarding what sources of evidence may be used to determine intelligence in non-human animals and elaborates a little on the use of these. Nevertheless, this answer should gain a great deal more marks if the writer had offered research evidence to support these sources of evidence.

There are six sources of behaviour from which we might gain evidence to show whether non-human animals have a ToM: imitation, self-awareness, social relationships, role-taking, deception and perspective-taking. Evidence for some of these behaviours will now be considered.

Kawai observed a snow monkey, called Imo, show novel problem-solving behaviour when she took her sweet potato down to the seashore and washed the mud off it. From this point onwards Imo washed all her sweet potatoes in the sea before eating them. However, some researchers claim that this may not have been novel problem-solving but simply an accident on the part of Imo who, on finding that the potato tasted better after accidentally dropping it into the sea did it again. Shortly after observing Imo wash her sweet potatoes Kawai observed that many of the other members of her troop also did this – evidence of imitation.

De Waal has provided evidence that chimps have self-awareness. He found that when they were shown their own image in a mirror they initially acted as if it were the image of another animal. However, a few days later, they appeared to realise that it was their own image as they began to show self-directed behaviour by using the mirror to groom themselves in, or to inspect parts of their body that would otherwise be inaccessible to them. This study may, however, suffer from anthropomorphism because the chimps may have just been using the mirror in a random way and not, as de Waal claims, to aid grooming, etc.

Evidence for role-taking has also been found in non-human animals. For example, Premack and Woodruff showed Sarah, a captive language-trained chimp, videotapes of human actors attempting to solve different problems, such as escaping from a locked cage or trying to obtain out-of-reach food. However, just before the film revealed whether the actor had successfully solved the problem or not the film was put on hold. Sarah was then given a choice of two photographs, one showing the actor performing an action that would result in successfully solving the problem and the other showing the actor performing an action that would not result in successfully solving the problem. Sarah consistently chose the photograph showing the actor successfully solving the problem. The researchers concluded that Sarah had shown role-taking behaviour because she had exhibited behaviours that indicated that she had assigned beliefs, desires, intentions, etc. to the human actor in the film. There is no real way of knowing if this was the case, however.

In conclusion then, it would appear that non-human animals do have intelligence, at least in terms of the behavioural evidence considered here.

Examiner's comments

The writer offers evidence of knowledge regarding what sources of behaviour may be used to determine intelligence in non-human animals and also offers research evidence to support these sources of evidence. However, while the essay clearly shows both knowledge and understanding, and uses appropriate information to answer the question throughout, it is weak on evaluation. Because of this a large proportion of the marks gained in this answer are for assessment objective 1. Consequently, while this essay has provided coverage of assessment objective 2 (e.g. 'This study may, however, suffer from anthropomorphism because the chimps may have just been using the mirror in a random way and not, as de Waal claims, to aid grooming, etc.') it should gain a much higher grade if it involved more analysis and/or evaluation. The overall mark for this essay would be about 8 marks for assessment objective 1 and 6 marks for assessment objective 2 – a grade C.

KEY RESEARCH SUMMARIES

Article 1

Rescorla, R. A. (1966) Predictability and number of pairings in Pavlovian fear conditioning, *Psychonomic Science,* **4: 363–384.**

Article notes

This article extends the evaluation of classical and operant conditioning in Chapter 3, where we considered the principles of both and found that one of the most important claims is that cognition is not involved in associative learning. Instead, behaviourists claim that learning is simply due to the formation of an association between a stimulus and a response and that repeated pairings of the conditional stimulus (CS) and the unconditional stimulus (UCS) in temporal contiguity are all that is needed for the association to occur. Pavlov *et al.*'s research also showed that the optimal pairing of the CS and UCS was forward conditioning, whereby the UCS was presented half a second before the CS as this resulted in the strongest CR. Furthermore, they showed that backward conditioning – whereby the UCS was presented after the CS – was not effective at all in that it typically inhibits the acquisition of an association between the UCS and CS.

It would appear that the above assumptions and findings on backwards conditioning may well be wrong, however, as research has shown that:

- Cognition does play a role in classical and operant conditioning as prediction appears to be a very important factor for the formation of an association between the CS and the UCS.
- Backward conditioning can be just as effective as forward conditioning for learning an association between a UCS and CS. Thus backward conditioning does not typically inhibit the acquisition of an association between the UCS and CS.

The following study is one of many by Rescorla that provides evidence to support the above two claims and refutes both Pavlov's claim that cognition plays no role in learning and Pavlov *et al.*'s findings about the inhibitory nature of backward conditioning.

Method and design: Laboratory experiment using an independent measures design.

Aim of the study: To show that classical conditioning only occurs if the CS enables the animal to predict the UCS and does not occur if the CS does not enable the animal to predict the UCS.

Procedure: Dogs were randomly allocated to one of two experimental groups and then proceeded as follows:

STAGE 1: Both groups of dogs were conditioned to jump (UCR) over a low hurdle in order to avoid pain in the form of an electric shock (UCS) that was administered to each side of the hurdle every twenty seconds. After learning to avoid the shocks each dog was removed from the hurdle situation and placed into one of two conditions for Stage 2.

STAGE 2: The dogs were now given a tone as a predictor of the electric shock, using either forward conditioning (condition 1) or backward conditioning (condition 2).

Condition 1: The dogs in this condition were presented with a tone just before the electric shock was administered – known as trace conditioning. The dogs quickly learned to jump the hurdle (CR) as soon as they heard the tone (CS). Thus the tone had become a CS that they could use to predict the occurrence of the electric shock and exhibit avoidance behaviour of jumping over the hurdle (CR).

Condition 2: The dogs were presented with a tone just after the electric shock was administered – known as backward conditioning. The dogs quickly learned not to jump the hurdle (CR) as soon as they heard the tone (CS) – if they had jumped to the other side they could predict that they would then receive the electric shock. Thus the tone had become a CS that they could use to predict the occurrence of an electric shock and exhibit avoidance behaviour of not jumping over the hurdle (CR).

Both dogs had learned to associate the tone (CS) with the administration of an electric shock, but the different temporal arrangements (i.e. trace vs backward-conditioning arrangements) with a different response – that is, jumping (CR in condition 1) and not jumping (CR in condition 2).

Consequently, it was the predictability that appeared to be the main determinant and not the temporal contiguity of the UCS and CS supporting the role of cognition in classical conditioning.

Many other researchers have shown that if the CS enables the prediction of a UCS then an association will be formed, but if the CS does not enable the prediction of a UCS then an association will not be formed (e.g. Kamin, 1969; Seligman, 1971). Indeed, Seligman (1971) has suggested that the CS act as a 'warning' signal to the animal that enables them to select the most appropriate response. In a series of studies Seligman showed that animals which have no reliable predictor of the occurrence of an electric shock act in a continually fearful way, whereas animals that do have a reliable predictor do not act in this way. Seligman thus concluded that the value of using a CS as a reliable predictor is that it informs that animal when it is safe to relax and when it is not, and hence enables the animal to be more effective in day-to-day survival in its environment.

Article 2

Tinbergen, N. and Kruyt, W. (1938) Study of the use of landmarks in homing behaviour in bee-killing digger wasps (*Pilianthus triangulum*). *Zeitschrift für vergleichende Physiologie* 25, 292–334. Cited in N. Tinbergen (1951) *The Study of Instinct.* Oxford: Oxford University Press.

Article notes

As we have seen in the first article cognition does play a role in associative learning in the laboratory; research has also shown that animals use cognition in the natural environment. This article widens our understanding of the way that animals learn in their natural environment.

Tinbergen, a highly renowned ethologist, carried out a number of important studies on digger wasps that clearly showed the role of cognitive learning in the natural environment.

The female of this species digs into the sand to form a complex burrow consisting of six to seven offshoot cells (Figure 5.1). In each offshoot cell she carefully lays one egg. She then exits the burrow and seals the entrance with sand until the eggs hatch into larvae (plural). At this point they will need to be constantly supplied with food if they are to survive. When the eggs hatch into larvae she returns to the burrow with food – a bee she has stung to death (hence the name!). On her return with the bee she then reopens the entrance to the burrow, drags the bee down to one of the cells to feed a larva (singular). When she has done this she then exits the burrow – once more sealing the entrance – and goes foraging for bees again. Each time she leaves the burrow she reseals the entrance and each time she returns she locates the burrow entrance exactly, takes another bee into the burrow, and continues doing this until, on average, each larva has received two bees daily.

Figure 5.1 **Female bee-killing digger wasp's burrow**

Thus, every time the digger wasp departs from the burrow and returns she has to find the exact location of the entrance to gain access to her young. Such a task is not an easy one as, apart from the fact that the burrow is built in sand and the entrance is sealed with sand, digger wasps usually nest in dense groups – there may be twenty or more digger-wasp burrows in a five-metre radius!

The big question is: how does the digger wasp learn to do this complex task? How does she learn the exact location of the entrance to her burrow and how does she distinguish her nest site from all the others in the vicinity? Tinbergen and Kruyt (1929) carried out a naturalistic observation study, followed by a field experiment, on the digger wasps living in the heaths and sand dunes of Hulshart in Holland in an attempt to discover the answer to this question.

In addressing this question Tinbergen and Kruyt realised that one of the first things that needed to be established was whether the digger wasps did in fact return to their own burrows. To establish this they marked each nest site and digger wasps with markers that identified which burrow belonged to which wasp and then observed their movements. Tinbergen and Kruyt's observations confirmed that the digger wasps always return to their own burrow.

Tinbergen and Kruyt then attempted to establish whether there were any cues in the environment that the wasps might be using as territorial markers to enable them to learn to identify their burrow site. They then recorded any possible territorial markers (e.g. sticks, stones, plants, etc.) that were around each individual burrow entrance. When they had done this they then placed a circle of pine cones equidistant around each burrow entrance and then observed whether the wasps would still return to their own burrow. Observations showed that they did. Tinbergen and Kruyt left these pinecone 'markers' there for a few days so that the wasps would have the opportunity to learn these. After a few days they then carried out their field experiment. They waited until the wasps had left on a foraging expedition and moved each circle of cones so that they were approximately one metre away from the entrance of each burrow and awaited the wasps return. Tinbergen and Kruyt wanted to see if the wasps could still locate the entrances to the burrows and, if not, what they would do. They found that on their return the wasps tried to locate the entrances to their burrows in the centre of the pinecones and not where the real entrance was located. It would thus appear that the wasps had learned to locate the entrance of their burrow using the pinecones as cues – and not using information about the entrance itself.

CONCLUSION

Tinbergen and Kruyt's study had clearly shown that digger wasps use local landmarks as cues for homing, and are consequently using cognitive maps to find their way back to their nest. Therefore it would seem that learning in the natural environment may well be much more complex than classical and operant conditioning explanations would suggest.

Article 3

Fiorito, G. and Scotto, P. (1992) Observational learning in Octopus vulgaris, *Science*, 256: 5455–5457.

Article notes

We considered social learning in animals in Chapter 4 of this book. One particular type of social learning is tutoring, and this was shown to occur in chimpanzees (Boesch, 1991). As chimpanzees are one of the animals most closely related to human beings it should not be that surprising to find evidence for learning via tutoring occurring. However, research by Fiorito and Scotto (1992) shows that the octopus also learns in this way.

Method and design: Laboratory experiments using independent measures designs.

Aim of the study: To establish whether octopuses can learn a skill from observing a tutor octopus.

Fiorito and Scotto (1992) have carried out a number of experiments to establish social (observational) learning in octopuses (*Octopus vulgaris*). In one such experiment Fiorito and Scotto conditioned octopuses to select one of two objects that were presented simultaneously and differed only in brightness – that is, a discrimination task. The researchers then allowed naïve (unconditioned) octopuses to watch conditioned octopuses demonstrate the discrimination task. The naïve octopuses were then isolated and presented with the discrimination task they had just observed a demonstrator octopus perform. Findings showed that the untrained octopuses consistently selected the same object as did the demonstrator octopus. Furthermore, the task was performed correctly, without significant errors, for five days. They also found that observational learning of the discrimination task was significantly more rapid than conditioned learning in the demonstrator animals.

In a different experiment Fiorito and Scotto conditioned octopuses to open a glass jar by taking a rubber plug lid off. The researchers then allowed naïve octopuses to observe the conditioned octopuses demonstrate the 'jar opening' on two occasions. The naïve octopuses were then isolated and presented with the jar-opening task. Findings showed that the naïve octopuses solved the same problem at the first trial without significant error, as compared to the five conditioning trials necessary for octopuses that had not previously observed the task.

The results of Fiorito and Scotto's experiments suggest that octopuses are able to learn both motor and visual discrimination tasks via observation of another octopus, and that observational learning of a conspecific performing the same task is significantly more rapid than via conditional learning.

CONCLUSION

Clearly, then, it appears that even those species that are less evolutionarily developed than humans and chimpanzees are more complex learners – much more complex – than classical or operant conditioning explanations would have us believe. It must be conceded, though, that the use of laboratory experiments means that such behaviours may not occur in the octopuses' natural environment. Yet they do suggest that octopuses may well use cognition in learning.

Glossary

Terms in this glossary have been highlighted in bold in the main text on first occurrence.

adaptation or **adaptive significance**   The process whereby an organism changes in order to survive in its given ecological niche (present environment); or a specific characteristic that enables it to survive in its given ecological niche.

altruism   Acting in a way that benefits others without regard to the cost or benefit to oneself.

anthropomorphism   This is when we attribute animals with human characteristics, such as experiencing the same emotions as humans (empathy, sadness, joy, etc.), when we do not know whether they do have the same experiences.

associative bias   The tendency to make association between a particular stimulus–response rather than any others that are as possible.

backward conditioning   In classical conditioning, a trial in which the onset of the unconditional response occurs before the conditional stimulus is presented to the animal.

behaviourism   An approach in psychology founded by John B. Watson in which observable, measurable stimuli and responses are observed without any reference to conscious or mental processes. (This approach argues that these processes don't play a vital role in learning.)

biological preparedness   A biologically determined readiness to learn some associations and not others.

conditional response (CR)   In classical conditioning it refers to the response elicited by the conditioned stimulus.

conditional stimulus (CS)   An originally neutral stimulus that through pairings with an unconditional stimulus now elicits a conditional response.

conditioned reinforcer   Something that through association with a primary reinforcer has become a reinforcer itself.

conditioning (or **associative learning**)   Learning an association between a stimulus and a response.

delayed conditioning   An experimental technique in which the presentation of the unconditional stimulus (US) is made after the presentation of the conditional stimulus (CS), but before the presentation of the US is terminated. For example, a bell may be rung *after* the dog is presented with its food just before the food is taken away.

ecological niche   An organism's position or function in a particular environment. Climatic variation, types of food available, sea or land, etc., are examples.

environmental niche   The nature of the environment in which an animal lives.

epiphenomenon   Consciousness regarded as a by-product of the biological activity of the brain.

ethology   The study of whole patterns of animal behaviour in natural environments, stressing the analysis of adaptation and the evolution of the behaviour patterns.

evolution   The process of orderly changes in the phylogenetic species that have been brought about by environmental and genetic changes.

evolutionary stable strategy (ESS)   A behaviour or strategy that continues because it cannot be improved upon.

external (ecological) validity   The extent to which the findings of a study can be generalised to the real world – that is, outside (or external to) the research setting.

extinction   In relation to classical conditioning, this term refers to the disappearance of a given response when the conditioned stimulus is repeatedly presented without the unconditioned stimulus. In relation to operant conditioning it refers to the elimination of a response by withholding all reinforcements of the response.

fitness/fittest   The degree to which an organism is successful in surviving in its ecological niche and producing viable offspring to ensure that the species continues. Thus an organism that has high fitness will have adaptive significance – that is, it will have inherited those characteristics which are best suited to surviving in that particular environment.

forward conditioning   In classical conditioning, a trial where the conditional stimulus precedes the unconditional stimulus and remains until the unconditional response occurs.

genetic transmission   Passing genes to the next generation through reproduction in one form or another.

genotype   The genetic material that an individual organism has inherited from the parent organism or organisms. It determines what characteristics an organism is able to develop.

higher-order or second-order conditioning   A form of conditioning in which the previously conditioned stimulus now functions as an unconditioned stimulus to condition a new stimulus.

inclusive fitness   The total measure of the various strategies that an animal may use to ensure genetic success. It consists of an individual's own personal fitness (i.e. getting one's own genes into the next generation) and the kin selection strategy which involves helping ensure the reproductive success of a close biological relative.

law of effect   The strength of a connection between a stimulus and a response is influenced by the consequences of a response.

law of exercise   The strength of a connection is determined by how often the connection is used.

law of recency   The most recent response is likely to govern the recurrence of the response.

law of reinforcement   The likelihood of a given response being emitted: if a response results in a positive consequence it increases the likelihood, but if it results in a negative consequence the likelihood decreases.

natural selection   Put simply, the proposal that those organisms that exhibit characteristics that are not adaptive will fail to survive long enough to produce viable offspring; consequently, such behaviours will diminish as the numbers of organisms exhibiting such characteristics diminishes. Those organisms that exhibit characteristics that are adaptive will survive long enough to produce viable offspring; consequently, such behaviours will increase as the numbers of organisms exhibiting such characteristics increases.

nature   The side of the nature–nurture debate that represents the influence of inherited characteristics on behaviour.

negative punishment   In operant conditioning, when a response results in something pleasant ending or being taken away.

negative reinforcement   In operant conditioning this refers to the termination of an aversive stimulus if the organism emits the desired response.

neutral stimulus   In classical conditioning this refers to any stimulus that does not naturally elicit the conditional response. In operant conditioning this refers to all environmental events that have no effect on a given behaviour at a given point in time.

nurture   The side of the nature–nurture debate that represents the influence that an organism's experience of their environment (e.g. diet, socialisation, education, etc.) has on behaviour.

operant   The label employed by B. F. Skinner to describe a response not elicited by any known or apparent stimulus.

operant conditioning   A type of learning involving an increase in the probability of a response occurring as the result of positive or negative reinforcement.

paradox   A contradiction or inconsistency.

phenotype   The set of observed characteristics an organism has developed – that is, those characteristics which environmental conditions have enabled the organism to develop.

positive punishment   In operant conditioning, when a response results in something unpleasant being presented.

positive reinforcement   In operant conditioning this refers to the receipt of an appetitive (desirable) stimulus if the organism emits the desired response.

primary reinforcer   A biologically significant appetitive (desirable) stimulus that directly satisfies an animal's basic needs (e.g. food, water).

primate   Any mammal that has a placenta, and typically has flexible hands, good eyesight, and, in the higher apes, a highly developed brain (includes apes, monkeys and humans).

punishment   The receipt of an aversive stimulus or the withdrawal of a desirable stimulus when an undesirable response is emitted.

response generalisation   The tendency for responses similar to the original conditioned response to be made in a similar situation. Thus the response is said to be generalised to the situation.

spontaneous recovery   The reappearance of an extinguished conditional response following a period of rest.

stimulus   Any event in the physical environment capable of exciting an organism's sensory neurones (i.e. the nerves of any of the senses such as smell, vision, etc.).

stimulus discrimination   Only emitting the conditional response when the original conditioned stimulus is presented and not when stimuli that are similar to the original conditioned stimulus are presented.

stimulus generalisation   The tendency to emit the same response to stimuli that are similar to the original stimulus.

temporal contiguity   Simply means occurring close together in time and proximity.

territoriality   The tendency to defend or protect one's space against invasion or attack.

theory of mind   An understanding that others possess mental states that accommodate ideas and accounts of the world that are different to their own, enabling the animal to make predictions about others' actions and motivation.

unconditional response (UCR)   Any response that is reliably elicited by an organism when an unconditional stimulus is presented without any previous training or pairing.

unconditional stimulus (UCS)   A stimulus that can reliably elicit a response without any previous training or pairing.

Bibliography

Baron-Cohen, S., Leslie, A.M. and Frith, U. (1985) Does the autistic have a 'theory of mind'? *Cognition* 21, 37–46.

Bernstein, I. L. (1991) Aversion conditioning in response to cancer and cancer treatment. *Clinical Psychology Review* 11, 183–191.

Boesch, C. (1991) Teaching in wild chimpanzees. *Animal Behaviour* 41, 530–532.

Brown, C. R., Brown, M., Bomberger, S. and Martin, L. (1991) Food-sharing signals among socially foraging cliff swallows. *Animal Behaviour* 42, 551–564.

Byrne, R. W. and Whiten, A. (eds) (1988) *Machiavellian Intelligence.* Oxford: Oxford University Press.

Cheyney, D. L. and Seyfarth, R. M. (1992) Abstract of 'How monkeys see the world'. *Behavioural and Brain Sciences* 15, 135–182.

Clutton-Brock, T. H., O'Riain, M. J., Brotherton, P. N. M., Gaynor, D., Kansky, R., Griffin, A. S. and Manser, M. (1999) Selfish sentinels in co-operative mammals. *Science* 284 (5420), 1640–1644.

Custance, D. M., Whiten, A. and Bard, K. A. (1995) Can young chimpanzees imitate arbitrary actions? Hayes and Hayes (1952) revisited. *Behaviour* 132, 837–859.

Darby, D. A. M. S. L. and Riopelle, C. L. (1959) In N. J. Mackintosh (1974) *The Psychology of Animal Learning.* London: Academic Press.

Darwin, C. (1859) *On the Origin of Species.* London: Murray.

Davies, N. B. (1978) Territorial defence in the speckled wood butterfly (*parage aegeria*): the resident always wins. *Animal Behaviour* 26, 138–147.

De Veer, M. W. and van den Bos, R. (1999) A critical review of methodology and interpretation of mirror self-recognition research in nonhuman primates. *Animal Behaviour* (3), 459–468.

De Waal, F. B. M. (1982) *Chimpanzee Politics: Power and Sex among Apes*. New York: Harper & Row.

De Waal, F. B. M. (1989) *Peacemaking Among Primates*. Cambridge, Mass.: Harvard University Press.

Eldredge, N. (1995) *Reinventing Darwin: The Great Evolutionary Debate*, London: Weidenfeld and Nicolson.

Faaberg, J. and Patterson, C. B. (1981) The characteristics and occurrence of co-operative polyandry. *Ibis* 123, 477–484.

Fiorito, G. and Scotto, P. (1992) Observational learning in Octopus vulgaris. *Science* 256, 5455–5457.

Fisher, J. and Hinde, R. A. (1948) The opening of milk bottles by birds. *British Birds* 42, 347–357.

Galef, B. G. (1992) The question of animal culture. *Human Nature* 3, 157–178.

Gallup, G. G. (1977) Self recognition in primates. *American Psychologist* 32, 329–338.

Gallup, G. G., Jr, Povinelli, D. J., Suarez, S. D., Anderson, J. R., Lethmate, J. and Menzel, E. W., Jr (1995) Further reflections on self-recognition in primates. *Animal Behaviour* 50, 1525–1532.

Garcia, J. and Koelling, R. A. (1966) The relation of cue to consequence in avoidance learning. *Psychonomic Science* 4, 123–124.

Goodall, J. (1965) Chimpanzees of the Gombe Stream Reserve. In I. De Vore (ed.) *Primate Behavior: Filed Studies of Monkeys and Apes*. New York: Holt, Rinehart & Winston.

Goodall, J. (ed.) (1986) *The Chimpanzees of Gombe: Patterns of Behavior*. Cambridge, Mass.: Belknap Press of Harvard University Press.

Gould, J. L. and Marler, P. J. (1987) Learning by instinct. *Scientific American* 256 (1), 62–74.

Gould, J. L. and Grant-Gould, C. (1994) *The Animal Mind*. New York: Scientific American Library.

Gould, S. J. (1989) *Wonderful Life: The Burgess Shale and the Nature of History*. Norton: New York.

Grier, J. W. and Burk, T. (1992) *Biology of Animal Behaviour*. Dubuque, Ia.: W. C. Brown.

Griffin, D. (1992) *Animal Minds*. Chicago: University of Chicago Press.

Hamilton, W. D. (1964) The genetical evolution of social behaviour. *Journal of Theoretical Biology* 7, 1–52.

Harré, R. and Lamb, R. (eds) (1983) *The Encyclopaedic Dictionary of Psychology*. Oxford: Blackwell.

Hauser, M. D. (1988) Invention and social transmission: new data from wild vervet monkeys. In R. W. Byrne and A. Whiten (eds) *Machiavellian Intelligence*. Oxford: Clarendon Press.

Hawaii Whale Research Foundation (http://www.hwrf.org/html/breach.html)

Hayes, K. J. and Hayes, C. (1952) Imitation in home raised chimpanzees. *Journal of Comparative Physiological Psychology* 45, 450–459.

Heinrich, B. and Marzluff, J. (1995) Why ravens share. *American Scientist* 83, 342–349.

Herbert, M. J. and Harsh, C. M. (1944) Observational learning by cats. *Journal of Comparative Psychology* 37, 81–95.

Heyes, C. M. (1998) Theory of mind in non-human primates. *Behavioural and Brain Sciences* 21 (1), 103–134.

Hölldobler, B. (1971) Communication between ants and their guests. *Scientific American* 224 (3), 86–93.

Holmes, W. G. and Sherman, P. W. (1982) The ontogeny of kin recognition in two species of ground squirrels. *American Zoologist* 22, 429–517.

Hoogland, J. L. (1983) Nepotism and alarm calling in the black-tailed prairie dog, Cynomys ludovicianus. *Animal Behaviour* 31, 472–479.

Howard, H. Elliot (1920) *Territory in Bird Life*. London: John Murray. (Reprinted 1978, New York, Arno Press.)

Jolly, A. (1988) *The Evolution of Primate Behaviour*. New York: Macmillan.

Jolly, A. (1991) Conscious chimpanzees? A review of recent literature. In C. R. Ristau (ed.) *Cognitive Ethology: The Minds of Other Animals*. Hillsdale, N.J.: Erlbaum.

Kamin, Leon J. (1969) Predictability, surprise, attention, and conditioning. In B. A. Campbell and R. M. Church (eds) *Punishment and Aversive Behavior*. New York: Appleton-Century-Crofts.

Kawai, M. (1965) Newly acquired pre-cultural behaviour of the natural troop of Japanese monkeys on Koshima Islet. *Primates* 6, 1–30.

Köhler, W. (1925) *The Mentality of Apes*. New York: Harcourt Brace.

Linden, E. (2000) *The Parrot's Lament*. London: Souvenir Press.

Lloyd, E. A. (1988) *The Structure and Confirmation of Evolutionary Theory*. Westport, Conn: Greenwood.

Lorenz, K. (1952) *King Solomon's Ring*. London: Methuen.

Mackintosh, N. J. (1984) The mind in the Skinner, *New Scientist* 2, 30–33.

Mateo, J. M. and Johnston, R. E. (2000) 'Armpit effect' distinguishes kin from strangers. *Proceedings: Biological Sciences of the Royal Society of London* 267 (1444), 695–700.

Maynard Smith, J. (1964) Group selection and kin selection. *Nature* 202, 1145–1147.

Maynard Smith, J. (1974) The theory of games and the evolution of animal conflicts. *Journal of Theoretical Biology* 47, 209–221.

Millikan, R. G. and Bowman, R. (1967) Cited in R. G. Millikan (1984) *Language, Thought and Other Biological Categories*. Cambridge, Mass.: MIT Press/Bradford Books.

Mumme, R. L. (1992) Do helpers increase reproductive success: an experimental analysis in the Florida scrub jay. *Behavioural Ecology and Sociobiology* 31, 319–328.

Nicolaus, L. K. and Nellis, D. W. (1987) The first evaluation of the conditioned taste aversion to control predation by mongooses upon eggs. *Applied Animal Behaviour Science* 17, 329–346.

Packer, C. (1977) Reciprocal altruism in *Papio anubis*. *Nature* 265, 441–443.

Pavlov, I. P. (1927) *Conditioned Reflexes*. London: Oxford University Press. (Reprinted 1960, New York, Dover.)

Povinelli, D. J. (1995) Panmorphism. In R. Mitchell and N. Thompson (eds) *Anthropomorphism, Anecdotes and Animals*. Lincoln: University of Nebraska Press.

Povinelli, D. J. and Eddy, T. J. (1996) What young chimpanzees know about seeing. *Monographs of the Society for Research on Child Development* 247 (61).

Povinelli, D. J., Nelson, K. E. and Boysen, S. T. (1992) Comprehension of role reversal in chimpanzes: evidence of empathy? *Animal Behaviour* 43, 269–281.

Premack, D. and Woodruff, G. (1978) Does the chimpanzee have a theory of mind? *Behavioural and Brain Sciences* 4, 515–526.

Rescorla, R. A. (1966) Predictability and number of pairings in Pavlovian fear conditioning. *Psychonomic Science* 4, 363–384.

Riopelle (1960) In N. J. Mackintosh (1974) *The Psychology of Animal Learning*. London: Academic Press.

Rose, S. (1983) In R. C. Lewontin, S. Rose and L. Kamin, *Not in Our Genes: Biology, Ideology, and Human Nature*. New York: Pantheon Books.

Ristau, C. R. (1991) *Cognitive Ethology: The Minds of Other Animals*. Hillsdale, N.J.: Erlbaum.

Russon, A. E. and Galdikas, B. M. F. (1993) Imitation in ex-captive orang-utans. *Journal of Comparative Psychology* 107, 147–161.

Savage-Rumbaugh, S. (1994) In S. Savage-Rumbaugh and R. Lewin (eds) *Kanzi: The Ape at the Brink of the Human Mind*. New York: John Wiley & Sons, Inc.

Seligman, M. E. P. (1971) Phobias and preparedness. *Behaviour Therapy* 2, 307–320.

Sherman, P. W. (1977) Nepotism and the evolution of alarm calls. *Science* 197, 1246–1253.

Sherry, D. F. and Galef, B.G. (1984) Cultural transmission without imitation milk bottle opening in birds. *Animal Behaviour* 32, 937–938.

Skinner B. F. (1938) *The Behaviour of Organisms*. New York: Appleton-Century-Crofts.

Skinner, B. F. (1969) *Contingencies of Reinforcement*. New York: Appleton-Century-Crofts.

Stammbach, E. (1988) Group responses to specially skilled individuals in Macaca fascicularis group. *Behaviour* 107, 241–266.

Stammbach, E. and Kummer, H. (1990) Cited in C. M. Heyes (1998) Theory of mind in non-human primates. *Behavioural and Brain Sciences* 21 (1), 103–134.

Thorndike, E. L. (1911) *Animal Intelligence: Experimental Studies*. New York: Macmillan.

Thorndike, E. L. (1898) Cited in E. L. Thorndike (1911) *Animal Intelligence: Experimental Studies*. New York: Macmillan.

Tinbergen, N. and Kruyt, W. (1938) Über die Orientierung des Bienenwolfes (philanthus triangulum Fabr.). III. Die Bevorzugung bestimmter Wegmarken. *Zeitschrift für vergleichende Physiologie*

25, 292–334. Cited in N. Tinbergen (1951) *The Study of Instinct*. Oxford: Oxford University Press.

Tolman, E. C. (1932) *Purposive Behaviour in Animals and Man*. New York: Century.

Tolman, E. C. and Honzik, C. N. (1930) Introduction and removal of reward and maze running in rats, *University of California Publications in Psychology* 4, 257–275.

Tomasello, M. (1996) Do apes ape? In C. M. Heyes and B. G. Galef (eds) *Social Learning: The Roots of Culture*. New York: Academic Press.

Tomasello, M. and Call, J. (1994) Social cognition of monkeys and apes. *Yearbook of Physical Anthropology* 37, 273–305.

Tomasello, M., Savage-Rumbaugh, S. and Kruger, A. C. (1993) Imitative learning of actions on objects by children, chimpanzees and enculturated chimpanzees. *Child Development* 64, 1688–1705.

Trivers, R. L. (1971) The evolution of reciprocal altruism. *Quarterly Review of Biology* 46, 35–57.

Visalberghi, E. and Fragaszy, D. M. (1992) Do monkeys ape? In S. T, Parker and K. R. Gibson (eds) *'Language' and Intelligence in Monkeys and Apes*. Cambridge: Cambridge University Press.

Westergaard, G. C. (1988) Lion-tailed macaques (Macaca silenus) manufacture and use of tools. *Journal of Comparative Psychology* 102, 152–159.

Whiten, A. and Byrne, R. W. (1991) The emergence of metarepresentation in human ontogeny and primate phylogeny. In A. Whiten (ed) *Natural Theories of Mind*. Oxford: Blackwell.

Wickler, W. (1968) *Mimicry in Plants and Animals*. New York: McGraw-Hill.

Wilkinson, G. S. (1984) Reciprocal food sharing in the vampire bat. *Nature* 308: 183.

Wynne-Edwards, V. C. (1962) Animal dispersion in relation to social behaviour. New York: Hafner.

Zentall, T.R. (1996) An analysis of imitative learning in animals. In C. M. Heyes and B. G. Galef (eds) *Social Learning in Animals: The Roots of Culture*. San Diego, Calif.: Academic Press.

Index